I'm NOT a celebrity
I am a Muslim
One woman's journey to a world of faith

by

Sahera Patel

ISBN: 978-0-9929955-7-7

Why not visit Sahera's blog on www.foreverfaith.co.uk ?

I'm NOT a celebrity

I am a Muslim

One woman's journey to a world of faith

by

Sahera Patel

ISBN: 978-0-9929955-7-7

Published by

i2i Publishing. Manchester.

www.i2ipublishing.co.uk

In memory of my dad whose wise words and guiding hand gave me strength and independence. His strength is now our strength.

All is forgiven. May God protect him with His Mercy and Love.

Ameen.

Foreword by Mohammed Amin

Every well written autobiography is a privilege, giving you the chance to see the world through the eyes of another person. Sometimes we bring our own preconceptions to the book, for example when the autobiography is of a well-known figure. In other cases, you know nothing about the person until you read their autobiography, as here with Sahera Patel.

Born in 1974 in Bolton, she was one of five children, mother of two and a former teacher. Despite her life being unexceptional, what she chooses to write about it provides insight into the experience of growing up in Britain in an immigrant family.

As I read it, I kept seeing commonalities but also differences between our life experiences.

Both of us are South Asian Muslims. She was born here while I immigrated but have no memories of Pakistan. Both of us are Muslims, have performed the Hajj pilgrimage to Mecca, and both of us had arranged marriages, deciding to get married after meeting our life partner just twice. However she interviewed about five times as many people as me before finding the right person! Reading how she went about husband hunting through the arranged marriage system should dispel many myths. It is also quite entertaining.

Conversely growing up in Manchester in the 1950's was

very different from Bolton in the 1970's, and being the eldest son with one younger sister was quite different to being one of five children.

Her book shows far fewer non-Muslim associations than I had and she mentions no intellectual interests apart from studying for her degree and religion. Perhaps most significantly, she is a woman!

Over the last sixty years immigration has changed the UK significantly. This book allows you to see life through the eyes of one relatively ordinary British Muslim of Indian origin. The better we understand all of our fellow citizens, the more harmonious our country will be.

I found the book very easy to read and always wanted to know what happened on the next page until I got to the end. I particularly recommend her experiences of Hajj, which were very consistent with my own. Especially the toilets!

Mohammed Amin, Chairman of the Conservative Muslim Forum and Co-Chair of the Muslim Jewish Forum of Greater Manchester.

Introduction

Writing a book was never part of the plan. Status, intelligence, resilience and downright determination are the characteristics of an author: people with time on their hands; silver spoon babies with no financial pressures and ambitious eccentrics who are fighting to stay out of the system. They are the heroes that have the potential to change people's lives with the power of their words – to provide a few hours of pure entertainment, taking us away from the mundane realities of life. I have always been the entertained: the customer in need of some escapism. Yet it was precisely this need to escape that first inspired me to cross to the other side - the thought processes involved in stringing words together to form coherent sentences, which in turn evolve in to flowing paragraphs, awakened my otherwise dormant, inactive brain cells. It provided me with a time out from the daily grind of work, home and family, awakening a deep, inner desire to tap in to the once creative, determined and academic me.

At the tender age of twenty-five I yearned for the absolute norm: kids, detached house, garden and cosy nights on the sofa with the love of my life. Single life offered some scope for happiness but with my religious morals and principles and my total dedication and loyalty to my parents, the only way I could achieve my mediocre goal was through marriage.

Fifteen years later and I have it all now: a lovely home, two adorable children, a husband to snuggle up to and a job that allowed me to leave behind the role of wife, mother and daughter in law. I am truly happy with the lot that's been handed to me, but human nature will always desire what it hasn't got. The 2.4 life-style inevitably draws one in to a cycle of routine: grocery shopping; mortgage repayments; school runs and the drudgery of cooking and cleaning. Single life, that offered a world of self-fulfilment and freedom, becomes a distant memory. However, unearthing my intellectual and academic skills that were so enthusiastically demonstrated over fifteen years ago could be considered a slight indulgence in self-fulfilment: a selfish desire that demands an escape from everyday routine for the process to be enacted and eventually, completed.

Becoming a serious author is not an ambition that many working mothers aspire to. Having completed this intrepid journey, there is no doubt that expressing one's thoughts and views with carefully considered words, does not come easy. It's a deep exploration of the mind. Only patience and persistence gets one from the beginning to the end, and life's little distractions provide countless barriers that have to be overcome. I begun this adventure hoping it would provide me with short bursts of escapism, but once I began writing, it quickly took hold as an ambition that had to be achieved - no matter how many years of my life it took to get there. Throughout the years I have strived to find pockets of quality time to produce some quality writing that would eventually lead me to become an author: a contender for the book shop customer looking for escapism and inspiration.

But how will I entertain the customer? How can I produce a page-turner with my level-headed, sensible life style? Have I found the answer to eternal happiness? Am I the first woman to achieve pure spiritual peace in a world that demands the female sex to split herself in to ten different identities? Not quite, but we should all look at our lives in detail - our history, look at the daily challenges we face, the people we meet, and the sometimes strange and unexplained thoughts in our heads. Life is full of choices, spirituality, emotions, hopes and dreams, be they achievable or not, that we choose to chase with vigour. Life provides us with challenges - challenges that are worthy of being broken down and explored. Every life matters and is unique in its trials and tribulations, its past and its future. This is my past, my present and a thought for the future. It provides an insight to a life that has had the privilege of experiencing a religion sandwiched by two very different cultures and the end product of this contradictory existence. It provides the experience of those emotions that we all feel everyday of our lives, a chance to relate, ponder, shed a tear and smile at our very own existence.

Throughout the book, I have included short 'Hadiths' (sacred sayings of the Prophet Muhammad, peace be upon him) to support my statements and beliefs and to highlight the stark contradiction between the teachings of Islam and the dominant nature of culture with its misinterpretations of the faith.

Sahera Patel

Chapter One

A tribute to humanity

Our existence is dictated by a life dominated by opposites. Without the harshness of cruelty we would not be drawn to the warmth of a kind heart. Without the agony of pain, our good health would be meaningless. Tears of joy only exist because we feel the pain of tears caused by misery, and without the certainty of death, the precious nature of life would be forgotten.

And it is with this certainty of death that my story begins.

Despite the desperately difficult nature of man's final rite of passage, a life of faith allows hope and peace to enter into one's heart even when the angel of death stands at his feet.

I begin my story at the end: at the point when my faith is my life and it can confidently provide me with an innermost peace at precisely the point in my life when I need it the most.

Time waits for no man, be it the coming of new life or the call of death. Last year, when my little brother unexpectedly found he delivering his third child on the dining room floor little did we know that the coming of this new life also marked the beginnings of the end for another.

With an adrenalin rush fuelling him, my brother strapped his two young children in the car and ran back into the house to get his full-term pregnant wife only to find her sprawled on the dining room carpet on the exact spot where we prayed whilst facing Mecca. She knew with absolute certainty that her third child was about to make its first appearance in the world. With the contractions fast and steady and the head partially exposed, my brother had no choice but to get down on his hands and knees and begin the mammoth task of delivering his own baby. There was no time to panic and no time to call for help: the labour was in full swing.

She pushed and he pulled as the baby gently made its way into the world. Within twenty minutes and after agonising moments of panic, pain and frustration, their eight pound son was born. My brother grabbed a coat and wrapped him in it, leaving the umbilical cord attached. He now had the opportunity to call for help and as the whole family made their way to hospital in the ambulance, the dining room carpet soaked in the remains of an exceptionally messy birth.

Mother and baby were given a clean bill of health and discharged from the hospital on the same day. My parents, who lived with my brother, were on their annual trip to India in an attempt to escape the harsh British winter so they missed the drama, but me and my three other siblings gathered at the house to hear first-hand the events of the day. We soon realised that the birth was a small miracle – a natural phenomenon without the complications that could have put my sister-in-law and our new nephew's lives in danger.

Humanity will be given moments such as these: moments where one's instincts are put to the test. Having faith in these instincts enables us to make decisions and react to situations that would otherwise seem impossible.

Natural instincts took over when my brother and his wife were faced with the challenge of giving birth with no form of intervention: self-belief dominated over any inklings of doubt or hesitation. This same faith kept us strong when we had to witness the pain and suffering of a life being consumed by the inevitable calling of death.

It was on his return from India in March 2012 that my dad informed us of his on-going stomach pains that were now becoming difficult to bear. One doctor in India had diagnosed a malignant tumour on his pancreas but later changed his mind, identifying it as benign. This uncertainty from an alleged professional raised our concerns, especially as the pain my dad was experiencing continued to trouble him. With absolute hope that there was nothing to worry about, we began the process in determining the nature of the tumour, through the local doctor. After a variety of blood tests, x rays and scans and some differing of opinions it was finally confirmed a few months later that the tumour was indeed cancerous.

Hope had always remained the dominant emotion in my heart and mind but this news tore away at the positivity that for many months had kept the word 'cancer' out of my world. The initial shock was a new, frightening emotion that forced itself to the forefront of my mind. Despite my best efforts to keep my emotions in check, during the first few days of hearing the news, the tears and pain overtook any rational steps forward.

There was certain illogicality about my dad threatening to leave the world. Old age was supposed to take him away gracefully – a natural end to a full life. Instead, I was left with thoughts of living a life without him. The painful possibilities ran through my mind as hope took a temporary step back: media portrayed images of thinning hair and a skeletal state forced their way in to my head, screaming negativity and serving only to deepen the pain. Moments of solace furthered my feelings of misery as I immersed myself in thoughts that centred around my own sense of despair.

As humans, we need time to absorb and accept life changing news. The fear, pain and self-pity that I was experiencing was a part of that process, however, the person central to our crisis was my dad and my first conversation with him about his illness opened up a door to my understanding of faith that praises one of the many attributes of humanity itself.

My dad said he had no desire to die. No sane, relatively healthy person would wish such a thing on himself, however, the reality of death was not in his hands. If Allah wished him to go back to Him then who was he to challenge the best of decision makers? My dad's trust in Allah was pure and strong, helping him to view his death as a positive part of his life. It was the calm, unquestioning nature of his faith that I admired. Without a clear prognosis, my dad had already accepted the possibility of meeting his Maker in the near future.

Allah says: "*Every soul shall taste of death. And We will test you with evil and with good by way of trial. And to Us is your return.*" [Quran - Sûrah al-Anbiyâ': 35].

But life is a valuable gift, and listening to my dad's acceptance of what lay ahead helped me to realise that my feelings were secondary to his needs and wishes. I allowed hope to seep back into my heart and my mum, my four siblings and I made a pact to remain emotionally strong, working as a team to do all we could to ensure my dad was happy and comfortable with any future decisions.

With an appointment scheduled at Christie's cancer

hospital in Manchester, the uncertain journey into the future was set. This first step was the beginnings of an emotional rollercoaster ride that would test our faith in God and humanity, revealing hidden depths of human strength and pushing our personal relationships to the limit.

The moment of truth soon came. Sitting in a small side room at Christie's, we listened as the doctor told us the heart breaking news: removal of the pancreas, which creates insulin in the body, would have been a possibility had the tumour remained on that organ, but more detailed scans revealed that it had spread in to the liver, making it inoperable. Further discussions with the doctors revealed that chemotherapy would simply be a means to prolong life by a number of months and was in no sense a cure.

There were no words that could soften the blow so we drove back home in silence, absorbed in our own thoughts and emotions. The finality of the diagnosis was difficult to process. My dad was far from the doors of death: he was still independent, walking and talking and firmly holding on to his strong personality. It was impossible to consider life without him, yet he had been given a prognosis of only six to twelve months with the help of chemotherapy and even less without.

The doctors informed us that the chemo would be un-invasive, having the function only to suppress the tumour rather than obliterate it. After some difficult deliberation my dad made the decision to go ahead with the treatment, basing it on the premise that our faith asked us to be pro-active with all our decisions in life whilst accepting the end result as one's divine destiny.

It was this unquestioning belief in the divine destiny that allowed my dad and all those around him to accept without question the nature of his illness. No-one was asking why it had to happen to him or what he had done to deserve such a serious condition. Because of the faith that we all carried in our hearts, the cancer, as contradictory as it sounds, bought with it hope and positivity. In Islam every moment of suffering is considered a moment where sins are forgiven and good deeds written. The pain that my dad was suffering was also erasing sins and making room for him in paradise. This belief, which we all shared with true conviction, gave us an incredible strength and enabled my dad to allow hope to enter his heart despite the pain and anguish of not knowing how his immediate future would pan out.

The Prophet (peace be upon him)said: *"No fatigue, illness, anxiety, sorrow, harm or sadness afflicts any Muslim, even to the extent of a thorn pricking him, without Allah wiping out his sins by it."* [Sahîh al-Bukhârî and Sahîh Muslim]

The chemotherapy sessions began in October 2012, three consecutive weeks for thirty minutes then a week of rest.

This process went on till the following March, suppressing the growth of the tumour whilst keeping my dad in relatively good health. There were no visible side-effects although he did suffer from exhaustion a couple of days after the chemo and had to be wary of contagious infections. The treatment seemed effective as the doctors at Christie's continued to report a steady blood count and a relatively constant visibility of the tumour through MRI scans.

When the initial stretch of treatments was completed the doctors gave the permission my dad desperately longed for to go abroad to India. They suggested that the chemotherapy had done all it could to stabilise the cancer and that further chemo at this point would be futile. We were all so overwhelmed by the happy news that he was healthy enough to take his annual trip to India; we temporarily dismissed the implied negativity. As we left the hospital, my dad laughed out loud, saying that the good news had given him so much energy that he could easily run out of the hospital as if he had the energy of five young men! It was one of the last times that we would see him smile with such vigour and joy.

The philosophy was always that our fate was in the hands of Allah, and that my dad would pass to the next world when He was ready to take him. Being given the good health to visit India, perhaps for the last time, was in itself a blessing. My dad was desperate to see his family back home and settle any debts, both in favours and financially, so the news that he was well enough to travel lifted his spirits and gave him hope that he had something to look forward to.

Within a few weeks, accompanied by my mum and older brother, my dad yet again found himself sitting on the front porch of the family home in the village where he grew up. This time however, there was a bitter sweet atmosphere as friends, relatives and local villagers visited him throughout the day to wish him well and offer him words of consolation. Many a times, it was my dad who assured the well-wishers that his fate was not necessarily one of despair and that doom and gloom was not the way forward.

My dad's first week in India maintained this positivity and his state of health reflected the hopeful atmosphere. He made the most of his renewed health by sorting out his financial affairs and repairing damaged relationships. Whilst talking to him on the phone, I remember telling him how his voice seemed to be performing acrobatic somersaults as it raced towards me. The cancer seemed to have taken a holiday too and for that week of respite, we all allowed the stress of the past few months to melt away.

But of course, cancer does not simply disappear. By the second week of his holiday, the old symptoms began to resurface, except this time they were returning with far more fury. Extreme heat, restless nights and changes in food and drink all added to my dad's frustrations. Dehydration continued to worsen as vomiting and constipation overtook him. The Indian doctors did what they could, and although Christie's had provided all the information required for them to act accordingly, without the security of a well established health system, it was clear to all of us that my dad needed to return home to a far more reliable network of care.

And it is the experience from the moment my dad was rolled out of the plane to the time of his passing that the real human story begins. Cancer is an unfortunate reality in the modern world, and I will not be the first to write about its devastating nature, but having the privilege of being by my dad's side throughout the last few weeks of his life gave me an insight to a man with unshakable faith. I was also given the opportunity to step into a world of deep spirituality that allowed a short glimpse of a reality that was far beyond anything of the earthly.

A few days after returning home, my dad was admitted in to Christie's hospital. They suggested clearing up the several infections that had found their way into his system in India and to re-hydrate him through glucose drips. Once the infections were cleared, they could focus on the cancer itself. This was going to take several days and, much to the annoyance of my dad, he would have to remain in hospital throughout that time. As it shall become clear later, my dad was not a man who could cope well with being told what to do, yet now he had no choice but to remain within the walls of his hospital room and allow the doctors to dictate his recovery.

From the onset, he told us that he didn't want to spend a moment in solace whilst in hospital and so, we organised a system of shifts between the five of us to ensure that at least one of his children was by his side throughout the day and night. His first few days in hospital were long and difficult. From over sixty years of total independence, my dad now needed assistance in walking, going to the bathroom and sitting up in bed. His frustrations were obvious and as his personality dictated, this extreme speed of physical deterioration did not suit his temperate nature. Despite his intelligence and understanding of all things spiritual, my dad had a short temper, especially with my mum. The pain and frustrations of becoming helpless in such a short space of time served only to exaggerate this side of his personality. We had to remain sensitive to this trait, as well as having to remind ourselves of the unimaginable pain and frustrations my dad must have felt at losing his independence within a short period of time.

After several days in hospital my dad showed no signs

of improvement, and so the doctors took the step of performing an MRI scan to monitor the development of the cancer. In our hearts, we already knew the results of the scan – and so did my dad, but the human instinct to hold on to the last remnants of hope fought back the negativity.

The human heart and mind can be torn apart by the extremity of emotions that run through them at times of hardship. I wanted my dad to live, yet seeing him in such a helpless state, overtaken by indescribable pain and a humiliating dependence on others, I was forced to question whether this was a better option than that of Allah removing the agony and taking him away.

But ultimately, as we all believed with sincerity, only God could take life away. My dad was forced to spend a few more days in hospital where they did all they could to help improve his health, but the moment soon arrived where we were given the news that would bury our worldly hope for my dad's life and move us forward to praying and hoping for a peace and happiness reserved for my dad in the after-life.

The consultant delivered the news of my dad's cancer spreading violently across his liver and lungs in the last few weeks. Her gentle voice and sympathetic tones attempted to comfort whilst remaining firm about the definite future facing my dad. A prognosis of two to three weeks was given and we were asked if that time was to be spent in hospital or at home. The choice was clear, and as we responded with the decision to take my dad home, she reiterated the definite impossibility of my dad returning to hospital once he was at home. He would be given the best of aftercare, but returning to hospital would, as in most cases, be futile, causing more pain and discomfort rather than relief.

The reality of my dad's death was now standing in front of us. It was heartbreaking: impossible to comprehend. As long as my dad was living and breathing, he was with us, and thoughts of him simply not being there anymore seemed ludicrous. But this was the certainty that we were to accept.

As we left the consultant, I slipped away from my family to gather my thoughts and attempt to control my emotions. It was the news that we were expecting, but the harsh reality of hearing the words confirming my dad's imminent demise were difficult to swallow. Throughout the consultation we held back the tears, remaining strong for each other, but once on my own, the tears fell uncontrollably. I stood near an open window, attempting to clear up the redness in my eyes but losing the battle as more grief poured out. I could accept what was happening, but I couldn't imagine a world without my dad's words of wisdom: a world without a father figure whose advice was sought by countless people and a world without the man who made me the strong, independent person that I am today.

As we made our way home with our dad from the hospital I looked to my faith to provide me with hope that God may keep my dad closer to me for longer and it gave me the strength to deal with the concept of death, accepting that the eternal world awaiting him was a truly peaceful and spiritual abode, far beyond anything that our earthly imaginations could perceive. Despite the beckoning of an end to a life, I sensed acceptance within me.

And acceptance was the oil that ran my dad's coping mechanisms from the initial onset of the cancer. Even at this stage, where he was bedridden and struggled to make conversation, he tried his upmost to express his gratitude towards Allah and held back on any form of complaint concerning his pain and discomfort. He could hardly eat or drink and our forceful attempts at feeding him frustrated his already challenged state of mind. Friends and family from all over the country came to visit, offering countless remedies but it was impossible for my dad to be enthused by their suggestions. As he progressively demonstrated his inability to consume food or drink, we became more panicked about his weight loss, leading to confusion and frustration. The nurses, who visited three times a day, re-iterated the inevitability of his loss of appetite but we found witnessing the speed of his deterioration painful and heartbreaking.

Remaining true to his wishes, we ensured that someone was by his side at all times. My shift began after the Morning Prayer – just before sunrise. In the month of May, this was around 5am. I felt blessed to have my shift fall at this time as it not only ensured that I did not miss the Morning Prayer, but it was also a time of day that was filled with serenity. After saying my prayers, I would sit myself next to my dad, who was now sleeping on a specially ordered hospital bed in the front room, with the Quran in my hand, ready to pray out loud in the hope that he could find some comfort in the words of Allah. My older brother would go home to bed and my shift continued until my little brother, who lived with my mum and dad, woke up. At this stage, my dad was constantly restless: the pain weakened then re-emerged as the pain killers moved in and out of his system. He had only small bouts of sleep and every time his eyes opened, we made it our duty to let him know that he was not on his own.

Sitting close to my dad, I would pray rhythmically, knowing that he could hear me but unsure if he recognised my voice. Occasionally, he would glance at me and the warmth of his stare would confirm that for a split second he knew who I was. I was constantly on the lookout for these shared moments of intimacy, looking to be taken back to the time when I took our bond of father and daughter for granted: when he was always going to be there, ready to share his advice.

My dad was from the old school generation: hugs and physical contact were rare, but human touch was now a much needed form of communication and holding his hand whilst praying provided comfort not just for him but for myself too. As I prayed I could feel the intensity of the Arabic words that I was reciting, despite not understanding them. The words oozed spirituality and I sensed that it was more than just my dad and me who were appreciating their divine beauty.

As I often witnessed, during the small hours of the morning, my dad would stare intermittently at different corners of the room, as if he was watching someone or something. These visions that seemed to appear before my dad are described in Islam as angels that visit a person for whom death is imminent.

"Say: 'the Angel of Death, put in charge of you, will (duly) take your souls, then shall you be brought back to your Lord.'" [Quran 32:11]

I could not interrupt these episodes of what I sensed as, divine intervention: these were private moments that were impossible to communicate in a world where such nonsense simply didn't exist. Yet in those small hours, when the soul of a dying man was being hugged with serenity and peace, it was the real world that seemed fabricated, meaningless and lost in its own determination to prove itself.

Unable to speak, the only time my dad did manage to utter a few words was when he was thanking Allah. As he lay in his bed, immersed in pain that only he could know, my dad would raise his right arm, stroke his head and say, "Oh Allah, I am grateful to you, oh Allah." This was one of the last things he said and they proved beyond doubt his complete faith in God. Many seek to question why God would cause such pain if He loved His servants yet I was blessed to see the answer come to life in front of me. It was because of The Divine Love that my dad was on his deathbed: the cancer tested my dad's faith to the limit, and as the illness consumed him, his faith remained unshakable. We all have to leave this world at some point and because of his strong belief and trust in God he left with an unimaginable purity. As my dad said, Allah knows best and having the opportunity to prove one's love for God by remaining faithful throughout hardship is a blessing and a preparation for the afterlife, however difficult it may be for all involved. Others who do not believe in a divinity find their own means of coping, but for those who have faith, and especially the followers of Islam, death can be just as much a blessing as it is heartbreaking.

The nurses and carers continued to provide an efficient, invaluable service but as two weeks passed of my dad being home, their roles began to diminish. My dad was no longer passing stools, he couldn't consume any form of food or liquid and a simple movement of the head was a struggle. We were warned that any attempt to force food or liquid down could cause an infection in the lungs, leading to pneumonia, however, my mum desperately tried to feed him, hoping that a few nutrients would result in my dad gaining some energy. My dad could no longer use any form of communication, yet it was clear from his face that he longed to be left alone. Loved ones wanted to hold on to him, keep him near and absorb themselves in the little that was left, but the signs were all pointing towards his departure from the ephemeral world. We had to learn to let go.

And having to let go came soon. On Tuesday May 14th 2013 I woke up just before sunrise as usual. After saying my prayers I took over the shift from my brother and began to pray aloud from the Quran. My dad's state of health was the same as it had been the day before. The morphine was helping to control the pain but his lack of food and drink intake and the gradual deterioration of his internal organs had completely taken away from him his former physical self and any signs of his former personality were diminished. His eyes still seemed to signal warmth when I looked in to them directly, and I often took this opportunity to talk to him: to tell him not to worry about the people that he was leaving behind. I was simply repeating his words, expressing how blessed he felt having five, loving children who flocked to be near him throughout his illness, and how my mum remained faithful to him all through her life despite the mistreatment she suffered from his hands.

I told my dad that he was one of the lucky ones, as he was leaving the world with a clean slate. His suffering had washed away his sins because of the purity and strength of faith that he demonstrated in his last days. I looked in to his eyes and told him to go to Allah without any worries about his children as we were all settled and happy. I reminded him about my little brother whose loyalty towards our mum would guarantee that she would always be living with him and not be left to fend for herself. Saying these words, which expressed finality about his passing, was difficult, but I managed to stay strong and hold back the tears in the hope that he found some comfort from them.

As I finished praying the Quran on the morning of the 14th, I sat on the couch next to my dad's bed, watching him whilst drifting in and out of sleep. At precisely eight o clock in the morning I noticed my dad's breathing change from regular to steady but short, quick breaths. As I stroked his forehead to let him know that I was close by, I noticed that his hair was moist with sweat. His limbs were straightened, which was unusual as in the last few days he was unable to straighten them on his own. His stomach, which had been swelled up with fluid, was now completely flat and his hands and feet were much cooler than normal.

Without any sense of panic, I woke my little brother up and asked him to call the nurses. As we waited for them to arrive, I continued to stroke my dad's forehead, looking in to his eyes that still seemed to be making an attempt at recognition. I had no doubt that my dad was breathing his last and this reality was tearing me up inside, yet I searched deep within me to fight the tears and stay strong for my dad. As Muslims, we all pray in the hope that the last words we say or hear would be the words that define a Muslim: *There is no God but Allah and the prophet Muhammad (peace be upon him) is his messenger*. Whilst looking in to my dad's eyes, I repeated these words over and over again, desperately keeping myself together.

Within ten minutes the nurses had arrived and with just a quick glance at my dad they confirmed what I already knew: my dad was going to leave us very soon. After calling immediate family, we sat around the bed, holding on to my dad's hand, praying. The nurses stood in the room, waiting. It was a surreal moment but despite the nearness of death, my dad's breathing remained steady and the atmosphere was calm and peaceful. Then the moment came: my dad simply took one breath and didn't take the next: there was no panic, no struggle and no resistance. One second his soul was with us, and the next it had gone. I glanced at the nurses and they nodded to confirm his passing. I stood up and kissed his forehead, saying the words *'to God we belong and to Him we will return'* and then stood back so that I could take in the fact that my dad was no longer part of my immediate world.

Absorbing my dad's passing was not difficult. I knew I would miss him terribly, but the immense spirituality that flowed throughout the experience of my dad's illness, and the faith that he demonstrated with every step of his suffering, confirmed with certainty my own faith and the belief that my dad was now in a much better place.

Chapter Two

Back to the beginning

Reaching that place where we feel comfortable in our own skin, where confidence overtakes doubt and hesitation, is not an easy journey. Human development is influenced by environment, by the people we meet and the challenges that we face in our daily lives. On the 9th of March 1974 I took my first step on the journey of life and it was many years later, after many lows and highs, that I found the real me.

My birth, although significant for a woman in traumatic pain, was not quite the momentous occasion that many of us perceive it as today. My mum didn't have the loving husband prepared to sacrifice the bones of his hand to help her get through the pain. He was aware that his wife could give birth at anytime, but being part of the process was never the intention. Neither was he traipsing the living room floor full of worry and excited anticipation. In my new world the father's role, in most cases, was diminished after conception. The deed done, it was now the mother's sole mission to endure the joys and pains of pregnancy, resulting in a perfectly formed little bundle of joy that was ultimately her responsibility, day in, day out.

For my mother, my birth came at a time when life was

becoming difficult. I was her third out of five successful attempts at procreation and although celebrations could have been appropriate, it seems that the atmosphere didn't call for an outward display of happiness. Not a single photograph exists of me as a baby or a toddler – which wouldn't be a concern if my older brother and sister didn't have countless baby photographs taken in a professional photo studio by professional photographers in a very professional manner! Time, money and maybe even happiness must have led to such extraordinary behaviour on the part of my parents. Yet by the time I came in to the world, such novel behaviour had been overtaken by the hardships of life.

Chapter Three

All hail England!

My parent's story is typical of those in their era. In the late 1960's demand for labourers was abundant but there was a huge shortfall in supply. The government actively encouraged immigrants to join a cheap labour workforce by relaxing the country's entrance laws. My mum and dad were part of the first generation of Indians who were about to face the challenges that arise when two cultures are forcibly fused together.

The culture shock of moving from a colourful country with warm, friendly smiles to concrete streets and cold faces was not an easy transition. After following a simple lifestyle, where a full belly and a roof over your head were the measure of a good day, they were thrust in to the nine to five life-style, where success was measured by the thickness of a wage packet.

My mum lived with extended family in the un-exotic surroundings of Nuneaton. She still lived a simple life, but without any of the pleasures that she took for granted back home: soaking up the sun whilst dangling her feet in murky water was now replaced by quick paced walks in the pouring rain; the rural village life, where the outdoors was more of a home than any bricks and mortar could be, was now replaced by four concrete walls that closed her in and imprisoned her. Back home, my mum was known as someone's daughter or friend, but now she was more valued for her wage packet. Every Friday she would present the little brown envelope, unopened, to the head of the family that she boarded with – close relatives that presumed rights over her money and her time. She spent the last of her teenage years working hard to earn money for others and fulfilling domestic chores that were taken for granted by those that commanded them.

My dad, like many other immigrants, was going through the same experiences as my mum and trying to adjust to a country that demanded hard work from its inhabitants. His brown wage packet also found its way to a relative's fireplace in the cotton town of Bolton. Back home there was talk of a promised land from the innocent and naïve Indians: England was a place where money was easy to come by and the British pound converted in to mega rupees. Relatives back home waited for their fortunes to be transported half way around the world, unaware of the sweat and tears that it took for those pounds to materialize in the first place.

A huge weight was put on my dad's shoulders. Not only was he expected to provide a regular source of income for his family in India, but his younger Indian siblings were also waiting for their lives to be 'bettered' as their elder brother miraculously created a life for them in England. Unfortunately, the duties of a son had to take precedence over any personal ambitions that were bubbling inside him. As an individual my dad had vision and determination. His intellect could have helped him to achieve far beyond his expectations. He was handsome, witty, confident and charismatic. However, he also had a mother in India who was expecting her eldest son to transform the lives of his family, even if it meant sacrificing his own dreams and hopes.

My mum's years as a cheap labourer were short lived. She was approaching an age where it could no longer be acceptable to have a single young woman in the house. If she remained unmarried questions would arise from the community about her validity as a potential suitor. They would doubt her credentials as a prospective wife, presuming that her inability to find a match stemmed from a murky past or a rebellious personality where she dared to express her personal needs and emotions. There was no question of choice for my mum. Marriage was an essential rite of passage and a cultural expectation that even my mum accepted as an inevitable process at a relatively young age. She talks today of the utter fear she felt, not knowing her future; the uncertainty of marrying a man that she hardly knew and the prospect of making these commitments to a virtual stranger when most of her family and friends were half way across the world.

Fortunately, one of her sisters, who had begun the process of immigration years before her, was now settled and married in Bolton. As the time for arranging my mum's marriage approached, my aunt invited her sister over to Bolton so that the business of hunting for a spouse could begin. After the turmoil of being uprooted from her family and community back home, she now faced the uncertainty and potential pitfalls of marrying a complete stranger.

Chapter Four

Marriage through a window

Fate had made its first move. My parents were now inhabitants of the same town. All that remained was for them to come upon a chance meeting and allow destiny to take its course. However, such scenarios were reserved only for the Bollywood movies - the image of the swinging sixties was not part of the Indian communities that were gradually building up around mills and factories. Although Indian fashions were incorporating bell-bottoms and mini dresses (as one outfit!) into their portfolio, the concept of free love and spiritual consciousness were shoved aside by the stronghold of Islam. The communities carried their faith, which was heavily intertwined with culture, over to a free-love Britain and remained determined to hold on to their moralistic, traditional way of life.

My dad had chosen to dabble away from this moralistic life style. He was enjoying the excitement and novelty of a new culture, providing a distraction from the demands of his Indian family as well as offering many temptations away from the teachings of Islam; however, these self-fulfilling days would now have to come to an end. It was time for him to accept the responsibilities of becoming a husband – to run a household with commitment and obligation. And so, his uncle, with whom he boarded, put the word out to the community that his nephew was on the look-out for a potential wife and that all proposals should come directly to him.

There was no question that they were both to have an arranged marriage: an arranged marriage in its most strict and traditional form. Compatibility was considered as a requirement only between the two families: religious standing and respectability within the community were investigated and assessed and if these criteria were fulfilled then the match was almost sealed. All that was required was for the man to find his potential spouse physically attractive and the deal was done.

This centuries old process of marriage, which historically stems across many cultures, dictated my parent's futures. They had no opportunities to discover if they shared the same level of intellect or had similar aspirations and hopes before they made the lifelong commitment. It was a form of arranged marriage that both of them readily accepted, despite the feelings of fear and trepidation that came with an uncertain future.

And so, weeks after my mum had moved to Bolton, she was made aware that a proposal from within Bolton was in the pipeline. Inevitably, her biggest challenge was overcoming the concept of marrying a virtual stranger, despite accepting it as the cultural norm. Her mind busied itself with numerous unanswerable questions about her future: how would she cope with the transition from emotional independence to shared emotions? Was she ready for the responsibility of running her own household? Having never had an intimate relationship with a man before, she feared that she would be a disappointment and questioned her own capabilities of fulfilling the role of a supportive wife. Her insecurities surfaced as she attempted to envisage an unknown future with a man that she was not to see until the proposal had been accepted.

And that day came soon, although my mum was blissfully ignorant of it. The man that was to decide her fate was hiding behind a net curtain near my auntie's house, waiting for my mum to walk past. Unaware that a potential husband was 'checking her out', my mum walked past the window as my dad lifted the net curtain and took a quick glimpse at her. It was those few momentous seconds that had decided the fate of my parents. My dad judged my mum as decent eye-candy, passing her looks as acceptable and therefore giving the final word that would move the proposal on to the next stage. There were no questions raised about education, individual beliefs or personal ambitions. Within a matter of days, my mum discovered that her engagement had been finalised. She had little input in her own future and she accepted the fate awaiting her: my parent's marriage had been decided through a glass window.

Ibn 'Abbas (may Allah be pleased with him) reports,

A woman companion of the Prophet came to him and said: "My father has married me away to one of his relatives without asking my opinion. I do not wish to stay with this man as his wife." The Prophet ordered their separation. When she realized that she was free and that she was no longer married to the man, she said to the Prophet: "I now accept what my father has done and I am marrying this man. I only did this so that women may know that it is not up to men to marry them away against their wishes." [Reported by Ibn Majah and Ahmad]

My mum saw her fiancée in passing: during family gatherings or in the neighbourhood whilst running errands, but they were never given the opportunity to spend time alone: never given the luxury of a private conversation or a shared moment of intimacy. Nerves and fear overshadowed any feelings of happiness for my mum on the day that was meant to be the happiest day of her life. She recalls being surrounded by strangers, very much aware that all eyes were watching her. As a bride, she was expected to remain subdued, with her gaze lowered and her emotions in check. As she sat next to my dad, her body shook with the fear of the future: the consummation of her marriage, becoming part of a relationship and forming ties

41

with people who already believed they had rights over her and her time.

But without the option to back out, my mum fought through her fears and made an attempt to build some sort of life for herself. In a matter of months the roles within my parent's relationship had become clear. They had similar backgrounds: family history; religion; upbringing and culture. One would expect that a couple with so much in common would engage in some intelligent, stimulating conversations and laugh over shared memories. Their recent experiences were virtually parallel and could be used as potential icebreakers for the unfamiliarity between them. But their destiny was not one of snug conversations and mutual adoration. Without the opportunity to assess each other's personalities and having the option of rejection taken away from them, they were left with the difficulty of successfully combining their personalities. I have no recollection of my parents openly praising each other or showing a small token of affection, even in the privacy of our own home. Their outlook on life; their understanding of faith and culture and their level of confidence varied immensely: my mum was a simple woman. Her ambitions lay in the home, striving for domestic perfection and building a social life within the local, Muslim community. On the other hand, my dad craved for far more. He yearned for intellectual stimulation and an ambition to move away from the psyche of the inward looking community. Their outwardly experiences were similar yet on the inside, my parents were two completely different people. Centuries of tradition, embedded in culture and contradictory to Islam, had dictated an incompatible partnership.

"And among His Signs is that He created for you mates from among yourselves, that you may dwell in tranquillity with them, and He put love and mercy between your hearts. Verily in that are Signs for those who reflect." [Quran - Sûrah Rûm: 21]

My mum's existence consisted of striving for perfection in her duties as a housewife and mother. Despite the constant struggles, she succeeded in raising me and my four siblings with love and affection; however, this praiseworthy ability to organise and run a household was strictly reserved for the home. She never demonstrated determination or independence outside the home. Even though she has lived for decades in the UK, like many other women who have lived with the same experiences as her, she has not mastered the English language. Not because of a lack of intellect, rather an absolute lack of confidence and ambition.

Yet I cannot blame my mother for her simple, unchallenged thought processes that led her to live a backseat life - accepting her fate without any degree of self-preservation. She grew up in a small village in India. Goats, bulls and mud huts were the main features of her environment. She never experienced modern technology and had no schooling beyond the primary level. From a young age it was instilled in her that her role in life was of housewife and mother. Living a life fulfilling one's own desires was not encouraged. The role models around her consisted of subservient wives and mothers who competed to cook the tastiest curry and dutiful daughters that accepted marriages arranged by their parents without challenge. The minority of women that did make a stand, and refused to fit the peg-hole were rejected by the community and lived lonely lives.

My mum's migration to England was not her decision. Neither was her marriage. She shaped her own destiny because of her lack of ability to demonstrate independence. But once one looks in to the history of her life and the lack of positive, independent role models during my mum's childhood, it is clear why women like my mother lived through such damaging, deeply painful lives.

So where did this leave my dad? His soul mate, life partner and shoulder to cry on, instead of filling the hole in his life, became just another frustration. He would go to my mum seeking consolation, sympathy and advice and would leave her without any sense of relief or reassurance. It was equally frustrating for my mum. Her perspective on life was far simpler than my dad's and the complicated, layered conversations that he was looking for were not within the realms of my mum's intelligence. To help ease his frustration, he looked towards my mum, only to find an insecure woman who misinterpreted his search for reassurance as a personal attack on her inability to help him. Each time they tried to have a mutually beneficial conversation; a lack of understanding would result in mutual pain. Eventually, they stopped searching for the warmth and security of a loving relationship: they simply became man and wife in the practical sense.

Chapter Five

First memories

My world opened up when I was old enough to venture
out into the neighbourhood and explore the lines of
terraced streets that filled my long days. I had begun the
process of collecting my own bank of memories: happy
memories, simple, innocent memories that epitomises the
childhood of every child of my generation who grew up
amongst rows of terraced streets. I see ice-cream vans;
sictoria; Milk-floats; auntie-filled rooms; wide legged
trousers and cheesy thingies.   I feel freedom, love,
acceptance and community. But mixed in with these
welcomed emotions was an underlying fear: an uneasiness
lingering in the background.

Like all my neighbours, and many other immigrants, we
didn't live in the most luxurious of homes. Rodents, slugs
and other unwanted pests shared our living space. Our
garden was the streets outside where we pushed our
imaginations to the limit to create a world of fantasy. We
used to while away a whole day near the river, taking in the
whiff of freshly baked bread from the Warburton's factory
and enjoying the innocence of childhood friendships that
retained purity without any barriers.

My mum was our security. Her priority in life was to

feed us, bathe us and clothe us. This blinkered vision of life was a blessing in disguise. She never had the desire for independence and thoughts of an escape from the drudgery were firmly locked away. She might have considered escaping her suppressive existence if she surrendered to her hidden inner strength – the natural determination within us all to escape mistreatment in search for a fairer existence. However, subservience and acceptance were the order of the day during my mother's era, and purely from a selfish point of view, her inability to make a stand provided us with an unconditional love throughout our childhood: a reliable source of affection in the form of our enduring mum.

Narrated by Abu Huraira.

A man came to Allah's Apostle and said, "O Allah's Apostle! Who is more entitled to be treated with the best companionship by me?" The Prophet said, "Your mother." The man said. "Who is next?" The Prophet said, "Your mother." The man further said, "Who is next?" The Prophet said, "Your mother." The man asked for the fourth time, "Who is next?" The Prophet said, "Your father." (Sahih Al-Bukhari Hadith 8.2)

My most vivid childhood memories conjure up images that contradict the pure innocence of childhood. I see a smoke filled living room with hairy, loud men sitting in a circle obsessing over playing cards. Bottles and glasses filled with alcohol are placed in front of them as they take small sips whilst concentrating on their hand of cards. I recall times when I would be in the room, unaware of the un-Islamic atmosphere that surrounded me: unaware of the struggle my mum faced having to deal with my dad and his friends who turned our home in to a place of gambling and drunkardness.

Dads don't lock their family out of the house in the freezing cold – or do they? Another vivid memory; there was a serious card game playing out in the front room and this time we were not allowed to mingle amongst the players. With my mum unable to control our disruptive behaviour, it seemed that the best place for us was in the back yard. After physically releasing his anger on my vulnerable mum for her inability to control us, he forcibly pushed us outside. We blubbered like pathetic children, clinging on to our bruised and battered mum, doing nothing to soothe her pain. Eventually, my dad's conscience got the better of him and he let us in, but only after the great card game had ended and he was ready to sleep off his drunken stupor.

Several times the gamblers would leave our makeshift casino having deposited random pools of vomit around the house. As my dad would fall into a deep sleep bought on by his extreme drinking, my mum would have to clear up the mess left behind. Feeling nauseous, she would use all her domesticity skills to get rid of the vomit, exhausted and infuriated with the situation.

And there eventually came a point when my mum had had enough. After several nauseating nights of cleaning up the aftermath of a night of debauchery, my mum decided to take the unusual step of looking for help from my dad's side of the family. Choosing a time when my dad was sleeping off a hangover during the day, she made a visit to my dad's uncle's house and informed him of his nephew's abusive behaviour, making sure that she had stressed her demeaning task of clearing up pools of vomit. The uncle responded quickly to my mum's complaints by making an impromptu visit to our house. He headed straight upstairs and physically dragged my dad out of bed much to his surprise. Next, his uncle pulled him down the stairs and slapped him hard several times across the face. Because of the requirement of respect and humility towards his elders, my dad remained quiet, listening to the many consequences he would have to face if he were to bring his gambler friends home again.

Despite the consequential abuse that my mum received for 'telling tales', my dad did stop inviting his friends over for nights of gambling and drinking – it was a small victory for my mum and a hard reminder for my dad that he couldn't continue to live the life that he was leading.

Fortunately, I was still very young when my mum was suffering the abuse. I recall the sense of fear and painful tears that flowed far too often, but my memory has been saved from the violent images of domestic abuse that my parents have mentioned in recent years. My older brother is merely one year older than me but his memory does conjure up unpleasant, distressing scenes. How he handled them at the time however, speaks volumes for the saying 'like father like son'.

His reaction to seeing my mum's physical signs that she had been abused one more time was one of indifference. It seemed that my mum was supposed to pull herself together by the morning, and so he would often tell her to get up and make him his breakfast. He was simply playing copy-cat: repeating the words of my dad in the same, domineering, unsympathetic tone of voice. It was only through maturity and an understanding that this was not the normality of existence in later life that he realised that things had to change.

Hadith quoted in Imam Ghazzali's Ihya Ulum-Id-Din, Marriage section:

"The most perfect of believers in faith are those who are the finest in manners and most gentle toward their wives."

Physical abuse was an unfortunate continuum in our

home for many years. Eventually, intoxication was no longer the only catalyst leading towards this abuse. A sober state, teamed with a bad mood, a tasteless curry or an infuriating comment was deemed a valid excuse by my dad's fickle conscience to raise his hand to his wife. Having to inhabit a home with such an erratic, unpredictable atmosphere, we quickly trained ourselves to maintain the peace by learning to assess the immediate mood. We could sense when my dad was tense, in need of a form of release. Subconsciously, we had become experts at analysing our parent's conversations – picking up on yet another dialogue between my parents where my mum was responding hopelessly to my dad's search for a refined, intelligent response. My dad's voice would crescendo as his frustrations continued to be fuelled by our mum. Once our radars picked up on the intensity of the moment we were quick to react, hoping to avoid the possibility of confrontation. Her rather simple, sometimes unreasonable responses to my dad's words would infuriate him so lulling her away from a guaranteed safety. As long as we caught the change in the conversation on time, she was safe. Without our intercession, she faced more of the domestic violence that she had by now accepted as part of her life. My mum seemed to have become the catalyst that drove my dad from reasonably calm to erratic and abusive.

I often question my mum as to why she suffered so

many years of abuse at the hands of my dad, knowing only too well the reasons why she remained the victim throughout her prime years. It's a long list of hopeless situations: no English, no job, no refuge homes, no community or family support, no confidence, no self belief, fear and fatherless children.

It was impossible for my mum to approach her sister – she had her own husband to answer to. Battered women simply didn't run back to their family after marriage – it was a culturally unwritten rule that abuse was part and parcel of married life and it was more dignified to suffer in silence.

There is no doubt in my mind that my mum could never have escaped from her terrible fate. Destiny plays a major role in Islam, but when oversimplified and confused with culture, its teachings become distorted. There is not a single action leading to my mum's beating that can be justified through the eyes of Islam as the Hadiths above demonstrate. The faith asks its followers to make an effort to shape their destiny, to fight injustices and only then accept the end result as the way that God intended. During my parent's era, Islamic education was at its basic level and one's destiny, however unjust, was to be accepted without question as this was considered God's will. Any attempt to fight the injustice of an abusive relationship was shunned by the community. My mum's personal devotion to her faith enabled her to find some comfort in her otherwise traumatic life. She believes that her sacrifice for personal happiness in favour of keeping her children happy will bring her the reward of a happy after-life and God willing, this will be the case. Culture, fear and a lack of independence restricted my mum's ability to step away from the abuse she suffered, but her perseverance has resulted in five well - balanced offspring who are very aware and humbled by her suffering.

Chapter Six

Happy memories

Before the uneasiness had crept in to our lives, our home did resonate with some sense of happiness. My one clear image of this happiness is a brown leather flat cap. It sat on my dad's head as he licked his finger to help him thumb through the piles of five and one pound notes in front of us. This short-lived financial freedom was a reflection of his ability to progress from the factory and develop his own business – a milkman business. Everyone had their milk delivered straight to their doorstep so there was abundant demand. He would drive around the neighbourhood in his red, open van delivering milk at the crack of dawn. Occasionally, we would be able to ride with him, holding on to the bar that ran across the back step of the van. Sometimes, we would accompany him to the houses of his customers, collecting the money for a week's worth of milk. These were happy, stress-free times, where money was readily available to transport to the relatives back home.

The demise of his business, which was a result of untrustworthy staff and mismanagement, was the trigger that led to the demise in his life. His mother, who awaiting financial booty back home, pressurised my dad and pushed the boundaries of desperation even further and once he found himself mixing in with the wrong type of crowd, he surrendered to all the temptations that screamed a life of hopelessness. With the pressures that were mounting up around him and the frustration that this caused, my dad found himself on a downward spiral that was taking with it all he valued and loved.

Luckily, the resentment and frustration that resulted in the physical abuse against my mum was never transferred on to us. We remained untouched, and despite the consistent threat of violence in our home, we felt secure that my dad reserved his anger purely for my mum. It was confusing and painful to witness a distraught mother, but like so many other experiences that one comes across in childhood, if they are a consistent part of your life, and there is no interference from the outside world, it becomes the norm.

In-between the bouts of abuse there would be many days of happiness: the gambling would stop; the screaming would stop, and our home would take on the form of normality. Employment was often the reason for these random bursts of peace. A steady stream of income and a slight easing of pressure from the family back home in India would instigate normal fatherly behaviour. We welcomed these bursts of happiness, as abuse had become the normality in our home and community. The tranquillity allowed us to form happy memories that also involved my dad.

Once, he asked us to select whatever we desired from a catalogue – money no object! This was an absolute luxury and a not to be missed opportunity to boast to our friends about our generous dad. I recall looking through the catalogue, absolutely mesmerised and overwhelmed by the countless choices. Eventually, I chose a mini Wendy house, 2 up 2 down with little pink flowered wallpaper and all the miniscule, life-like furniture included. My older sister, a confident and sometimes intimidating sibling, chose some roller skates with which she cruised the terraced streets for many years later. We shared mutual feelings of excitement and anticipation as our super gifts arrived and temporarily changed our lives for the better.

Another memory that has always lingered in my mind, although insignificant compared to the experiences of my mum but yet strangely powerful, happened when we were all clock watching, waiting for the start of mosque. My dad was in a bad mood. The curry wasn't up to the required standard. It was cold outside and his useless children continued to leave the living room door wide open as they traipsed in and out. Eventually the five of us settled on the settee, dressed in our Burkhas and Topees. My dad, who by now was extremely irritated, was sitting on the opposite settee attempting to eat his salt-less curry. His frustration with us eventually took over and he got up, walked across to us and slapped my four siblings one by one gently on the cheek. Fortunately I was at the end of the sofa, and his conscience must have got the better of him before he reached me. I have a clear memory of my dad laughing later on, and telling me playfully that I had escaped his hand. That moment is an extremely fond memory of mine. I felt like we had a little secret between us, and that I had won the prize.

I also share many genuinely happy memories with the other children from our neighbourhood. We had an incredible freedom, and a simple concept of happiness. Fresh air and friendships filled our days. Stranger danger was non-existent and there was no pressure to wear, buy, say or play the latest gadget or attitude. No complications, just simple fun: zooming through streets on the bike - no helmet; rounders on the street - even in the dark; playing jacks with a friend - only cost 50p; a game of sictoria - just finish drinking the coke can and we have our target; buy 3 packets of crisps with 10p pocket money, crush them up and they taste much better; Vera in the sweet shop - 10 kids at a time, no problem; launderette trips for my mum - big, scary white lads; pretending to be a rock star – dancing, performing; the old man at no. 73 - haunted. The list goes on. A happy, freedom filled list - a time when fun was independent, not a quick bid on e-bay by your parents. It is these memories that convince me of a happy childhood, despite the pain of my mother's suffering

But independent fun didn't last forever. The age of technology was coming, and my dad fell victim to its lure straightaway, much to our delight. We were the first home in the street to own a colour television and we quickly became the talk of the neighbourhood. Within days, visitors to our home quadrupled! Our home became a techno - colour spectacular, free of charge cinema! The curious neighbours felt no embarrassment at entering our home and enjoying a freebie and there was no sense of superiority on our part. It was an unwritten rule that front doors were never locked and all the neighbours were free to enter.

Next came the BBC computer. My dad had really outdone the neighbours this time. His theory of spending the money you have got, and the money you haven't got was being put into practice. He had discovered hire-purchase and suddenly objects of desire that seemed far out of his reach had become accessible. The freedom filled list of childhood pass-times crumbled as the metamorphosis into the modern day childhood began.

Chapter Seven

Community spirit

The face of our community was changing rapidly as I entered the great, free British education system. Indians back home were incredibly envious of this system, and rightly so. What most of us take for granted was only a dream for the families that worked hard just to get the food on their plate. The inevitable changes were clearly visible as the white community began to leave and the Muslim invasion began. The corner terrace with the converted attic became an impromptu mosque and the great British butcher, whose cuts of pork and unblessed meat that were rank with sin were now replaced by the Halal butcher. Familiarity and security were leaving the white residents of the neighbourhood and the Muslim residents were doing all they could to make themselves feel at home. It's a trend that society continues to demonstrate today, and although integration works as a theory, in reality, too many compromises and sacrifices have to be made. Rather than bringing communities together, a culture of resentment and misjudgement can be created. Education, respect and a willingness to be a part of the society as a whole seem the way forward for all cultures.

My local primary school had a majority intake of Muslim

children by the time I graced its intimidating doors. Living in a majority Muslim community with an extremely limited experience of the outside world resulted in virtually no interaction with the white community, apart from those in authority. The few experiences I did have as a young child, I often found intimidating and harsh.

One of these experiences was during one of the many laundrette trips that were a routine part of our lives. My mum would wash the clothes in the kitchen sink and we would be sent to the laundrette on the main road to rinse and dry them. We were around the age of 8 when my younger sister and I started our independent laundrette trips. To prevent our ear piercings from blocking, my mum used to thread some cotton through the piercing and tie a knot: bizarre but extremely practical. It stopped the piercing from blocking up, and was an affordable alternative to three sets of earrings that were very likely to get lost on more than one occasion.

And so, we dragged our wet washing to the laundrette with our fashionable cotton earrings dangling proudly from our ears. We were both very timid when we were younger, and it must have shown. A couple of teenage white lads were hanging out at the laundrette taking advantage of the warmth created by the huge, steaming dryers. They were very pleased when their source of entertainment walked through the door. They waited for us to sort our washing out, then, just as we sat down on the wooden slatted benches, the onslaught began: extremely racist remarks, demeaning comments and invasion of personal space. They flicked our ears, and laughed at our embarrassing alternatives to earrings.

The whole world closed up on us. We felt vulnerable and exposed. Completely powerless, we sat through the insults till our washing was dry. That was the first time that my sense of belonging was challenged, and I didn't like it: suddenly, I was different. My presence offended these boys and they had no desire to hide their disgust.

Our skin was a much darker shade than theirs, and our clothes were brighter and more interesting. We spoke some 'bud, bud, ding, ding', as they described it, and we gave off a slight whiff of curry as our mum was cooking when we left the house. These English boys were older: their sense of belonging and sense of power far outweighed our position in the hierarchy of society. Silently, we took the insults without any reprimand and left the launderette a little more confused than the last time we came.

Over the years, as similar experiences taunted my life, I realised that the problem didn't lie with me – it was in the thwarted minds of the offenders. It was their sense of belonging that was being threatened. They saw a community bound together by tight morals and a genuine care code where *Love thy neighbour* wasn't just a quote in the bible. As the Western communities moral systems were crumbling, the Muslim communities were getting stronger. It was intimidating for people with insecurities about their own culture to see such a united community, and I believe it is this vulnerability that caused such hostile reactions from certain groups towards Muslims.

This pattern of behaviour is still evident today. Halal curries, dhoti trousers, idle gossip, religious gatherings, Islamic education and the desire to belong are all factors which encourage Muslims to live near other Muslims. Inevitably and understandably, non-Muslims move out as they begin to lose their own sense of belonging. There is no hiding from the fact that we feel most comfortable with people that share our views on how our lives should be lived. It is only now that I appreciate how important this build up of community was to me, and how it influenced my thoughts, attitudes and helped to build my identity.

Chapter Eight

Where did all the gold go?

In between the gambling, my dad worked as a takeaway chef, and a taxi driver. My mum made Christmas crackers at home, fitting in a change of a pooey nappy, and conjuring up a sheep brain curry in between. I vividly remember lines of Terylene nappies on the washing line after my mum washed each one in the kitchen sink; our hero.

Thanks to my dad's intimidating uncle, our home was losing its identity as the meeting place of immoral misfits. The smoked filled rooms, and strange voices were less frequent. Our house felt cleaner, as alcohol ceased to fumigate the rooms, and cigarette smoke no longer poisoned the air with such intensity. My dad claimed to have consumed an excess amount of alcohol during these trouble filled years, and he still continued to gamble, but in the casinos – a more acceptable environment. Unfortunately, my mum remained an easy target: the abuse was less frequent; nevertheless, it was still an ugly, unnecessary part of our lives.

Slowly, the Indian uncles and aunties started rolling in to the terraced jungle. Immigrants were invading our home as my dad fulfilled his duty as the oldest, British son. With the people, came the politics, and with the politics came the many disputes that further distanced our desire for happiness.

As the oldest sibling, even during his childhood days, my dad was making sacrifices. As a young teenager he had a trail of seven siblings following him around. His mum relied on her oldest son to fulfil the household chores and to quieten the rumbling stomachs. Life for a victim of violence was difficult. She needed time to recover after the beatings from her oppressive husband, and her oldest son had to take on the responsibilities that she couldn't fulfil. So my teenage dad waited until the seven little siblings satisfied their hunger, servicing his own pangs of hunger with what little food was left at the end of the meal.

Now the seven siblings were all grown up. They had heard about the riches that lay waiting in England and were spurred on by an ambitious mother, who envisioned a better life for her children. My dad was expected to be the miracle worker who would create a reality that matched their misguided fantasies, but within days of their arrival the walls of illusion crumbled to the ground.

I recall the frustration they felt, as it dawned on them that they would have to work to survive. It demanded physical strength and enough determination to leave a warm bed only to face hours of monotonous labour. Early starts and late finishes were routine and the bitter cold was a constant reminder of what they had left behind. There was pressure from the family back home to evenly distribute their precious earnings and an expectation to pay their own way. The prospect of an easy ride was quickly diminished as the reality of an immigrant's life dominated over their fickle visions of luxury.

And together with their broken fantasies, they faced a man in my dad that was no longer the playful, nurturing older brother that lived in their memories. He was now a difficult, unpredictable man to live with. Anger and frustration were constantly squeezing the joys of life out of him and his calm demeanour had manifested in to a projection of fear. His two brothers and a sister, who had now successfully entered into the UK, witnessed the anger within him and so, never dared to challenge him. The lack of communication and expression of true emotions resulted in a broken down system where bitterness and resentment festered and gnawed away within all those involved.

However, the one weakness that had always crippled my dad continued to dominate him: his consistent respect towards his mother. Despite her inability to communicate any form of affection or appreciation towards the many sacrifices he had made in his life, he still remained loyal to her needs and wishes.

According to Maulana A.E.M. Yusuf, a religious scholar

of Bangladesh,

Muhabbat Idtirary: Natural love such as love for parents, children, own brothers, and sisters, etc. Such love comes naturally and no matter how extremely a person is upset or angry with them, his love will not decrease.

Matrimonies between the Indians and their British cousins sealed their futures as permanent residents of the great UK. They became part of the two up two down culture and began the process of integration into a community that was determined to maintain its identity. Younger generational cousins randomly appeared as my extended family grew at an unprecedented rate.

As age overtook my grandparents, the balance in their relationship shifted as my grandmother became more vocally dominant. Her insistence upon a better life for her children, no matter what the cost to her elder son, became a mantra that my granddad could no longer challenge with his fists, and so, she moved towards a more dominant role in their relationship.

My grandmother visited Britain regularly to assess the progress of her offspring. Naturally, she chose to reside in the oldest child's home, which added to my mum's already heavily burdened day. Having to contend with a frustrated husband was a challenge in itself, but now she had to deal with a mother in law who presumed an absolute right over her.

The wife in Islam is absolutely under no obligation to take care or serve her husband's parents or family; the duty and ultimate responsibility that the parents are served and well cared for is entirely upon the direct offspring of the parents. But if the wife, of her own will and choice, wishes to go over and above her prescribed duties and in her benevolence serves the parents and/or family members of her husband, she would be doing the extremely meritorious deed of 'Ehsaan' (that which Allah loves) and Allah Subhanah absolutely loves those who do 'Ehsaan' or deeds over and above their prescribed duties. If a husband is blessed with a wife who does 'Ehsaan' and serves his parents, he should be extremely grateful and thankful to her for her superb gesture of benevolence and kindness. (Quote from Wister, Wisdom towards ethics & righteousness, Islamic search engine)

My grandmother lived in our home with her eyes wide open. She was fully aware of the abuse that my mother suffered at the hands of her son, yet there remained an attitude of acceptance – even a hint of entertainment. Abuse was no stranger to my grandmother, and to witness her daughter in law's suffering seemed only to confirm her acceptance of a reality that was thwarted beyond recognition. A secret pleasure of power bubbled inside her as her past was played out in front of her, albeit by her own flesh and blood.

The close-knit community and the claustrophobic nature of the terraced streets ensured that nothing stayed behind closed doors. Disputes between the uncles and aunties made their way towards our home and disrupted the already fragile environment that my siblings and I constantly strived to maintain. Clutching at straws, my grandma would inevitably conclude that my dad was to blame for all the misery. Where was the life of financial freedom that Great Britain promised? From her point of view, my dad had failed to buy the happiness that she craved for her offspring.

The vicious cycle of blame, frustration and abuse continued. Loyalty and expectations cornered my dad into an existence of subservience towards his mother. The dictated nature of his life resulted in the total eradication of freedom and spontaneity, which led to the abuse; a crazy, paradoxical way of remaining sane.

As my dad's British siblings settled in to a life of monotony the remaining Indian siblings back home were becoming restless. They had yet to reap the benefits of the English pound and were becoming impatient with the lack of monetary support that they felt was their absolute right.

Gradually, hard earned funds were collected and transferred to the family back home - the family back home that would never realise that the quality of their lives far outreached that of their British relatives. Within a short space of time, a mini-mansion arose from the Indian soil and it seemed that my dad was fulfilling his mother's dreams. The cost of these dreams was heavily laden with sweat and tears. There was no appreciation of the hours of work or awareness of the constant gambling or the pain the human punch bag had to endure for their materialistic gains.

This pattern of behaviour was not unique to my family. Many of the immigrants who found themselves in Britain had the same expectations from their families back home and most of the Indian benefactors remained ignorant of the life of drudgery and monotony that their loved ones were experiencing, not to mention the neglect of first-generation, British born Muslim children who were not getting their fair share of parental attention and affection.

Chapter Nine

School days, mosque days, happy days

Primary school offered its own intimidations that challenged my timid, non-confrontational persona. The constant activity, forced conversations with overtly confident peers and high expectations from the teachers led to an introduction to school life that I initially found difficult to adjust to.

P. E in the school hall consisted of thick, dangling ropes and oversized trestle tables that were awaiting an attack by over excited children, but my enthusiasm for all things physical was lagging far behind. From an early age I became aware that my strengths lay in the academic subjects: each piece of work, whether it was Art, English or Mathematics, I completed with motivation and confidence. Although my intellect didn't reach the status of top dog, it was a comforting thought to know that I could handle whatever was thrown at me without an underlying sensation of failure creeping in to my psyche.

At parent's evenings, my mum would sit through ten minutes of listening to my teacher's words - words that were to her, complete gibberish! I translated my teacher's words as best as I could. Even though the gibberish was always positive, any negative comments would not have led to negative consequences. My mum was indifferent. She came because she had to, and I know it pleased her to know we were doing well, but no action would have been taken to try and reverse a poor attitude. There were far more pressing problems, such as family politics, and financial strife to deal with. Our natural academic skills during primary school made life at home a little simpler, but they were never a priority in a household that struggled to find a real sense of peace from one day to the next.

'Renaldo! What a wonderful name! And who thought of that?' I felt proud as the head teacher called out the runner-up of the Easter egg competition held annually at our school. It was my neighbour's entry, but I had thought of the name. I put my hand up slowly, feeling happy, shy, nervous and excited all at the same time. He congratulated me on having such a wonderful imagination, and as the whole school turned their heads to see who it was that had provided the creativity, I held my head up high, bursting at the seams with pride.

Eating samosa sandwiches on a narrow boat named Kemajuma:
I was in the top five of a class competition, and the incredible, unique prize was to spend the day on our teacher's narrow boat with her family. It felt like another world: transported from the terraced jungle to a peaceful

haven of lightly splashing water and warm smiles. I remember my utter disbelief as my teacher announced the prize and the magical thoughts that dripped gradually in to my consciousness: how could something so wonderful happen to me? Was I really going to be a passenger inside a boat? I recall standing at the top edge of the narrow boat, attempting to steer it, astonished that someone was willing to hand over the controls to me. The prize was an opportunity to feel the world away from my home and family: a brief moment of escape.

There was however, no escape from the four walls of the mosque. Corporal punishment was close to extinction in the school system, but at mosque, slaps, sticks, physical pain and humiliation were everyday occurrences. Our regular mild beatings were not monitored or curbed - they were an established form of discipline which was a tradition carried over from the mosques in Pakistan and India.

By the age of five, each Muslim child began a daily routine that would involve hours of studying from dawn to dusk. Thus by the time we left our studies at an average age of twelve and emerged from the terraced jungles, we would be super intelligent human beings, who could speak two languages, Gujerati and English, fluently. We could also read a language we didn't understand (Arabic), and speak the dialogue of Bollywood (Hindi.) But of course, in every generation, there are the naturally gifted, the drifters and the hopeless. Unfortunately for my generation, it was the lack of encouragement, praise and opportunity that pushed the drifters towards the hopeless. Many families had to deal with challenges as faced by my own, and the children's aspirations were very much bottom of the list of priorities.

My first mosque was a converted corner terraced house with an attic. On the outside it was an ordinary looking house with a sign above its door, but inside, there was no mistaking its identity, although the main entrance was not the most welcoming of sights or smells.

The first thing you would see as you entered was the communal lavatory. These were the two outdoor toilets, hole-in-the-ground style. Although they were disguised well with tiled exteriors and a chain flush, naked, they were just holes in the ground. Unfortunately, holes in the ground do not perform the job of flushing away bad smells very well, and I still remember the filthy stench that remained after each flush. I tried to hold my breath on the occasional times when I couldn't wait but it wasn't humanly possible to remain breathless for such a long time. There were always queues and teasing outside as each person's leftovers were commented upon: we were 250 children, from the very young to the teenager, trying to make the best of a very smelly situation!

The entire ground floor was packed to the brim with

young children rocking back and forth as they recited their 'Sabaq' or lesson for that evening. I can still hear the echoing sound of 100 children robotically repeating Arabic words that meant nothing to them. But yet, there was something quite magical, peaceful and warm about it. It made me feel safe and secure - innocent expressions of peace and love to a God that none of us yet understood.

Abu Hurairah relates that the prophet Muhammed, Peace be upon him, said:

No people gather together in one of the houses of Allah, reciting the Book of Allah and studying it among themselves, without tranquility descending upon them, mercy enveloping them, the angels surrounding them, and Allah making mention of them amongst those who are with Him.

(Imam Nahawi's 40 Hadith, chapter 1, hadith no. 36)

On the first floor was the boy's only room. As the floors of the mosque ascended, so did the age of the occupants. By the time you left the ground floor, segregation became a necessity. The boys were privileged as they were taught in the congregational prayer room. The carpets were designed as prayer mats, and the men would gather there to recite their five daily prayers. For the girls, aged 8 and above, there was the attic. A large, echoey room that was full of the promise of girly adventures, vicious, organised fights and daily bouts of uncontrollable laughter.

The empty coffins were stored at the back of our attic classroom… a perfect trigger for our overworked imaginations to fire up out of control. The gory ghoulies and vicious vampires would be waiting for us as we made our way up the wooden staircase. They would watch us, waiting for us to leave, so they could haunt the mosque in the dark. Our young, creative minds would take us to scary, intimidating places all because of the practical problem of having no other space to store the empty coffins.

We would all be gathered around the coffins by half past four. Our teacher wouldn't arrive till at least quarter past five…he was always fashionably late. Then, on the occasional fight night, the two willing participants would present themselves and take to their appointed corner, each brimming with confidence. Someone would keep watch. The starter bell would ring and the two girls would scratch, kick, push and shove to their hearts content. The audience would calmly enjoy the show, so as not to disturb the worshippers below. Then a warning…back to your places quick! We would rush back on the carpet, 'Patlas', or short benches in front of us, with our prayer books and the Quran open in front of us. By the time our teacher entered we would have created the perfect picture of dedicated learning.

It would be insulting to the hardworking teachers of today if I referred to our mosque man by that title. He wasn't unique. Several 'teachers' failed to fulfil their role as educators during a time when Islamic studies were still in the foetus stage. The job of maintaining discipline, inspiring and teaching with depth and understanding, and earning the respect of their pupils was far out of their reach. They had a mammoth task to complete.

In an ideal world, I would have liked to have understood the Arabic language, read it, written it and have had the confidence to speak it. Only then would I have been able to appreciate the true meaning of the Quran. For an average man, with little education, who couldn't understand or speak Arabic himself, it was an impossible task. In reality, he had to educate over 30 girls, of ages 8 to 13 for 10 hours a week on a very minimum wage. Those ten hours were mostly taken up by the 'teacher' listening to individual girls recite part of the Quran, often, with his eyes only half open. Occasionally he would enthral us with a public bogey picking session, and on those difficult days, we would be treated to the delightful sight of observing our teacher snoozing – his head gently drooping down then sharply rising up as he made a bizarre snorting noise, only to fall right back in to his snooze: clearly not a job to be taken too seriously.

And it was this laid back atmosphere that made mosque more of a social occasion than a place of education. We spent hours sharing sweets, swapping stories and whispering about boys. One entertaining pass-time (as long as YOU weren't the source of entertainment) was to watch our teacher punish a student for breaking a rule. This didn't happen very often as he was rarely alert enough to notice, however, a loud voice, the consumption of sweets, swearing or an inability to recite the Quran, on occasion, led to a show of punishment that was deserving of an Oscar.

Other forms of punishment, such as being hit with a ruler on the hand and getting slapped lightly on the legs were akin to the corporal punishment laws. A quick slap on the hand with a ruler or cane was the most common form of entertainment. One girl was especially good at not complying with the demands of the punisher. She would put her hand out hesitantly, constantly pulling it back just as the cane came down. Her little voice would squeak with fear, as the punisher became more and more frustrated. Eventually, he would hold her hand as the stroke of the cane lashed on to her fair skin, making it blotchy and red with pain. She would wince and walk away, whilst the captivated audience struggled to hold back their giggles: a truly entertaining event.

Chapter Ten

Growing up

My innocent and naïve view of the opposite sex was beginning to change as I approached the end of my primary school years. I used to dismiss their existence, labelling them as annoying creatures who only seemed interested in playing football, but then one particular boy caught my attention.

I considered his appearance unique: not that of a typical Indian boy. Fair skin, soft, floppy hair and sparkling eyes made him stand out from the others. Despite this obvious handsome exterior, he rarely made conversation with the girls in school, including myself. I knew nothing of his personality, having never exchanged a single word with him, yet he flooded my thoughts with a private obsession that filled my monotonous days with secret moments of fantasised first kisses.

This obsession was however, a deep secret, so it was no surprise how devasted I felt as an anonymous love letter addressed to my secret obsession was accusingly waved in front of me. For an eternal fifteen minutes, a group of girls stalked me in the playground as I repeatedly proclaimed my innocence. It was only the ring of the bell that saved me from the utter humiliation I felt at having my secret discovered. The feelings I harboured for him were so new and strange that I would never have confided in anyone at that time, let alone take the risk of writing it all down. I was confused, feeling sick to the stomach. The injustice of publicly being wrongly accused so many years ago still rises to the surface when I think of it today, and despite the seemingly petty situation, at the age of ten it felt like my whole world had been torn apart!

As my primary years came to an end, I became more conscious of my outward appearance. Sparkly cerise earrings, with a matching necklace and cerise shoes are my first ever memory of feeling truly fashionable! Everything was carefully co-ordinated, even the black and white striped bat-winged jumper, which I thought matched beautifully with my blinding cerise outfit! I was so proud of my hexagonal reflecting earrings, and couldn't wait to show them off on Eid. At the age of 10, Eid was one of the best days of the year. For the grown-ups, the build up to Eid was slow and exhausting. A whole month of fasting preceded the event: long summer days without food or water drained away their energy, but for children, it was the one day of the year when they were guaranteed brand new clothes, and plenty of spending money.

Three packets of cheesy thingies, mashed up of course, from Vera's sweet shop; a sparkly plastic ring, too big for my skinny fingers and a quarter of delicious strawberry sherbets making the top of my mouth sting… a heavenly shopping list, awaiting execution.

Every Eid, my mum had to prepare iconic Indian dishes for her in-laws. It was a presumed duty that she would be responsible for the cooking and it took many years before the extended family released my mum from the annual responsibility, sharing the labour intensive work that was involved in producing an oversized pot of perfectly cooked biryani.

Every Sunday night was 'English night' which usually involved fish n chips for dinner. My mum would peel a bag of potatoes, and fry the thin slices in an Indian style wok. Thin slices of fresh cut cod would appear in the kitchen every Sunday night and my mum would cover it with homemade batter. Then she would bath us in the sturdy black and white suite, one by one. The pear shaped Vosene bottle would be empty by the time she lathered five filthy heads. We would rush into the bedroom in front of the Cannon triple slate heater, wrapped up in our towels. After a vicious rubbing down it was straight to bed ready for school the next day. Definitely a job for a super mum!

The mysterious case of the five pound note

One day, my mum and dad had left a five-pound note on the big, mahogany mantelpiece that loomed over the gas heater in the front living room. (Maybe it wasn't looming, but from the eye-level of a child, one could be excused for mistaking it for a magnificent piece of woodwork, dominating over the old record player and the big box television in the corner.) The five-pound note was weighted down with a mini Taj Mahal, to ensure its safekeeping. But it wasn't safe for long.

We all stood accused of thieving from our very own family: a shameful, degrading act that deserved severe punishment. But no one was prepared to confess. Individually, we were adamant that we weren't the culprits, but somebody was, and my dad was determined to identify the guilty one out of the innocents.

So what line of investigation did my dad take? : Threats to our pocket money? Being grounded: a loss of privileges? Or a firm reprimand that put fear in our souls and forced a confession? Not at all! My dad had a much more traditional method that would ultimately prove who the thief was. He asked my mum to pour some mango pickle oil in a cup, and presented it to us.

We were all asked to dip one of our little fingers in the oil one by one, not knowing the rules of the game or how we could win. Each finger came out looking yellow and greasy, except for my little brother's. His little finger came out a darker tone of yellow, almost orange. My dad gave him an amusing look that seemed to accuse him of the evil deed. He started protesting his innocence, as the rest of us looked on, unsure if this meant he was in for a severe punishment or whether this was just a bizarre source of entertainment for our dad.

No action was taken and my little brother never did produce the five pound note, proving that the whole episode was a slightly worrying game that my dad played on us to entertain himself and perhaps, to teach us a lesson about honesty. Whatever his motives, for many years afterwards we believed that the oil test would discover any attempts we made at deceit, and so my dad's scaremongering had achieved its purpose.

Another incident that my little brother was undoubtedly guilty of happened when he was still bumbling around in recyclable nappies. The portaloo that hung between his legs had reached its maximum capacity. It was heavy, almost dragging itself across the carpet, and marble like poo was trying to make its way out. One little morsel managed to find its freedom, and landed in full view of my little brother. The living room was dimly lit, and, as any sugar craving, innocent toddler would do, he bent down and picked up the tempting ball of 'chocolate' that was screaming to be eaten. We quietly observed the proceedings, holding back our laughter, awaiting the grand finale. He didn't disappoint. The poo reached his mouth, and was quickly followed by a desperate choking scenario, where my brother attempted to get rid of the foul tasting poo. From a child's point of view, nothing could be more repulsive and therefore more entertaining than watching someone eating his own poo!

With only one or two years between us, and an obvious few years between 'the mistake', the five of us grew up together. My older siblings gave me the confidence to move on from one challenge to the next: a new set of classmates, a fresh bully or making-up with a friend when you are the one at fault. Each small challenge seemed like an impossible mission at the time, but one after another, they were accomplished, and as the years progressed, the challenges become increasingly complicated and difficult to overcome.

Life at home was slowly fighting its way towards the path of normality. We were all growing up, developing individual personalities, opinions and behaviours. My dad must have sensed this, and consequently toned down his wayward behaviour, though not obliterating it altogether. He had grown accustomed to relieving stress on a human punch bag, and he was not going to give it up that easily.

Chapter Eleven

A taste of the real world.

Towards the end of my primary years, I had met and bonded with the person who was going to be my best friend for the rest of my life: Sameena. We connected. Our minds seemed to work on the same level, our thoughts often meeting in the middle. Another close friend, Razia, also joined our little group and we became destined to share our high school troubles and joys together.

My first year of high school was spent at the 'annexe', devoted to first years only. It was an old, square building with a garden at its centre. Ignorant, unpleasant creatures that preyed on the vulnerable and made every attempt to hide their insecurities by adopting an intimidating, confident persona infested the building. My path had crossed with a few of these strange creatures during my younger years, but I had never seen so many in one place: all competing to reach the ultimate goal of 'school cock'.

Sameena's family had moved up in the world. They were one of the first families in our community to escape the terraced jungle, choosing to leave the pungent smell of spicy curries for the less imposing aroma of fish n chips. Sameena's bus journey to school was more civilised then ours, as she used a public service, open to all members of the human race, however, the bus journey that Razia and myself took was exclusively reserved for students. It was full of scary, intimidating characters that seemed to prey on our differences. They had an admirable determination to make our daily journey a living nightmare, a determination, that had it been steered in the right direction, could have made a positive impact on their lives.

The first day of high school: I almost looked like any other schoolgirl: a smart black jumper with the school logo on it, white collars sparkling against my brown skin and a grey knee length skirt. But it wasn't just my brown skin that pronounced victimisation. Like every other Muslim girl, I had to cover my legs. We wore 'skinny' black or grey trousers under our skirts to demonstrate modesty. The normality of this form of dress was embedded within me yet within minutes of my first ever and worst ever journey to high school, this exterior sign of my culture and religion became an embarrassment and an apparently ludicrous statement of fashion. I still feel cheated and de-moralised when I think about the immediate power my ignorant peers had over me. They made me question what I was, who I was and what I represented. In the long run, their ignorant attitude initiated my journey into the discovery of my personal identity. Their insults, jibes and racist comments made me stronger and more confident as a person. It was the instant affect that was difficult to comprehend and even harder to retaliate against.

Razia and I stood in the queue at the bus stop, butterflies dancing in our stomachs, ready to get on board the orange double-decker bus. We had heard many horror stories, and were warned in advance not to go upstairs. As we clambered on to the noisy, crowded bus, the driver said the words that we had been dreading…"off you go up them stairs; there's plenty of room up there."

Our hearts pounded as the rowdy crowd of school kids involuntarily pushed us up the curved staircase. As soon as our heads bobbed up to the first floor of the bus, our sense of smell was triggered. The stench of cigarettes filled the air, and dull grey smoke clouded the view. There were no double seats left at the front of the bus, nor were there any in the middle of the bus. There was no question of us parting company so we took the brave decision to sit on the very last double seat preceding the infamous back seat. We felt vulnerable, sensing the lions around us awakening, having spotted their prey and planning on their attack.

Avoiding eye contact seemed to be the best option, so we looked at the floor and stared out of the window alternately. Neither of us wanted to talk. Our only thought was to reach the end of the journey. At the halfway mark we allowed a little relief to creep in, but the sense of hope was premature… someone from the back seat slapped the top of our heads with their school file which was then followed by roaring laughter. Then the group of girls who occupied the back seat came towards us and began to pull at our clothes, mocking the 'skinny' trousers that were to become the height of fashion within their own lifetimes. They flicked their fingers on our brown skin, making fun of its colour and pulled at our long, lovingly tied plaits. As they tried to force their lit cigarettes in to our mouths, attempting to spark a reaction, we remained silent and stared straight ahead of us. "Why are you not saying anything?" they kept asking, getting more and more frustrated and angry as we dealt with the unfamiliar taunting by ignoring it. For those long five minutes, our world closed in. Nobody was going to rescue us – it was only ourselves that could save us from the effects of the constant enduring of humiliation and degradation.

Finally, it was over. The worst bus journey of our lives ended as we stepped out of the smoky torture chamber only to walk in to a mysterious, challenging environment where our insecurities, fears, hopes and dreams were to be realised and tested to their limits.

Chapter Twelve

A Year of Separation

We were in the annexe hall and three hundred students, some more nervous than others, waited for their names to be called out. We were discovering who we would spending the rest of the year with. I desperately prayed that I would be with my two best friends, or at least one of them. Whatever the outcome, I didn't want to be the one who ended up alone. A selfish desire, but at such a vulnerable age, the security of a real friend played the role of a comforting childhood blanket.

My two best friend's names were called out together. They followed their form teacher, and I was left in the hall with a handful of students. As we trailed behind our teacher, I frantically searched around for brown skin. Only brown skin would understand my skinny trousers, appreciate my humble humour and share my numerous unwanted confrontations with white skin.

I entered the classroom and made a beeline for the one brown face eagerly staring back at me. To be fair, her skin tone was lighter than the average brown face, which automatically pushed her up a few levels on the Asian beauty scale. It didn't matter if her features were absolutely average; the light skin guaranteed her admiration from the generation above us.

We began to have a conversation, if one could call it a conversation. We talked, but it didn't mean anything. I wasn't stimulated, moved or motivated. She didn't inspire me, or share the same emotions that I was feeling. In fact, I don't think she was experiencing any emotions. This was the point in my life when I realised I had a certain snobbery about friendships and conversations, which probably explains why I never had a big circle of friends. I craved a childhood form of intellectual conversation, where there was a purpose, and an emotional attachment. At the tender age of eleven, such 'intellectual' conversations only took place between me and Sameena. We put the world to rights with our pompous talk of Islamic practices and our simple perceptions of how the political systems operated. Each of our ignorant offender's psyches was broken down bit by bit, carefully analysed and boxed up in our many self-made categories of the condemned human being...Typically, we also enjoyed reading Smash Hits, and relished hearing the latest gossip in school!

And so it was. For a whole year, I only saw my true friends during break times and lunch. We shared our classroom experiences during these moments. Some experiences were happy ones where we felt involved and integrated with the other students: I recall a group of us being chased by some boys on the playground, and my unusually triumphant response of kicking one of them in the balls - a loud burst of painful moaning was followed by several cheers of congratulations.

There was the shared experience of the annexe bully. I have never since met anyone like her, although I am sure there are plenty of aspiring wannabes. She had a tiny frame of a body, a head that was shaped like an egg and a thin, squeaky voice. Yet it was this almost lizard-like creature that was terrorising all the first years. It wasn't just the brown faces that found her intimidating. Every girl and boy in the annexe remained cautious when she was in their presence.

My only personal encounter with the bully, which thankfully did not involve any violence, was a very short, revealing conversation I had with her as we were walking along the straight-line corridors of the annexe. With her lackeys walking behind her, she asked me if I liked her new haircut. Being a meek, non-confrontational child, with no desire to be involved in a situation, I answered the question exactly how she knew I was going to answer it...'yes'. Then I walked as fast as I could away from her, without giving the impression of running for my life!

As soon as I caught my breath, in keeping with my true intellectual nature, I analysed our 'conversation', deciding it must be desperately sad to be in a situation where you would never get an honest answer from anyone because they were simply too scared that you would beat them up.

Our lunch was served in an outbuilding; a glorified shed that accommodated hundreds of hungry children indifferent to their surroundings as long as their hunger was satisfied. In those days, school dinners were served on real ceramic plates, and portions were generous. The gorgeously unhealthy chips and thick, saucy beans were slopped on to our plates with enthusiasm. Big, fat filled slices of cake with deliciously lumpy custard ended a perfect meal.

Once a week I would end up in a room full of big square solid worktops, with vices, planes and saws as standard and chunks of random wood scattered around ready to be violently attacked by inexperienced carpenters. The smell of dead trees and clean shavings filled the already densely thick air that was pulsating with fear at the deep, intimidating voice of the woodwork teacher. He bellowed at ignorant students who mishandled chisels and stared at the vices like strange, ancient artefacts. Yet within that hard exterior there was a soft, mellow character that occasionally reared its endearing head through his apathy towards the completely useless but hardworking student - just like me.

My first ever woodwork production was a totem pole come lamp stand. I meticulously carved small trenches out of the long cuboid of tree, sanding and rubbing till the wood was as smooth as my eleven-year-old skin. The simple design that proudly coveted my lamp cowered behind the gloriously chiselled patterns adorning the rest of the lamp stands, but I could tell by that twinkle in our teacher's eye that he was just as proud of my achievement as I was.

Chapter Thirteen

Faith

I quickly realised the value of true, meaningful friendships as I continued my first year making new friendships that I knew would not last. My most useful, fulfilling conversations continued to flow only with Sameena. Her response to my mum's experiences was that of calm, deep reflection that only confirmed my own realisation that my mum deserved nothing but respect for all that she suffered and was still suffering.

Much of the physical abuse transformed itself into emotional abuse, although he still lost self-control on occasions. During the day, whilst my dad was at work or asleep, depending on the phase that he was going through, the atmosphere would be calm, happy and peaceful, but in the evenings it changed. We became more alert, observing and assessing my dad's behaviour. A playful comment directed at us would send tingles of relief through our bodies: nothing to worry about. But there were times when he would throw a deathly glare at my mum just because she said something that he considered unreasonable. It was these evenings when we had to transform ourselves from innocent children to the domestic abuse police. Our mum was the potential victim - we knew how she could avoid the wrath of my dad, but she was incapable of withholding her comments often saying the wrong words at the wrong time.

Our first mission would be to separate them. We could not take it for granted that they could have a civilised conversation without erupting. Once accomplished, we would closely monitor the occasions when they had to meet, and be ready to take action if there was a hint of change in the atmosphere. Usually, quick separation avoided confrontation. Sometimes, it didn't, and it was on these occasions that even our policing didn't avoid a crime being committed.

I was coming of age. Once I turned twelve, all the Islamic rules and regulations would become obligatory. Without perfect role models, this was going to be a challenging task. My dad rarely performed his daily prayers, and chose to ignore the rulings on domestic abuse. Although the foundations were there through mosque and the strong moral uphold of our community, the daily practice of praying five times a day was always going to be a difficult one to uphold. My mum tried. She had many prayers that needed to be answered, confused thoughts that needed to be rested and painful memories that she wished would go away.

It took me many gradual years of self-taught meditation and deliberation to discover the power of true belief.

Without faith, my mum may have struggled to come out from her traumatic experiences, yet some would argue that it was because of her faith that she accepted her destiny and my dad justified his behaviour. Looking at the history of my parents, it seems that religion is partially to blame – but it is the misinterpretation or even a total lack of desire to learn about the religion that has caused an infusion of religion and culture that does not reflect the true teachings of Islam. It is too easy to blame God for the horrendous human acts that destroy individuals, communities and countries yet it is rare to find a person of faith blaming God: it is often people without faith that point a finger to the heavens, a paradox, as one cannot blame something that in their minds doesn't exist...the blame has to go to humankind itself.

Faith guides you through life. My mum is not unique in her experience. Women throughout the world suffer yet not all of them believe in God. They will search for and find their own way to console themselves and move forward. Some women never move forward. With the help of God, unquestionable faith and strong determination my mum managed to survive and continue living without becoming depressed, disturbed or constantly resentful towards those around her.

Faith provides peace of mind, and an internal calm that makes your journey through life less turbulent and more accepting of what lies ahead. In some form or another, we all have faith. Our hearts and souls seem to possess a fighting spirit that holds on to hope. My mum has been rewarded for her suffering by seeing all her children settled and happy. Some would interpret this as a message from God; to suffer hardship within your own life and reap the rewards later in life through the ones you love. Non-believers may say that it is all a part of the circle of life and one must learn how to move on. What I do know is that my mum found her faith a constant, positive part of her life amidst the fears and uncertainty that threatened her everyday existence.

One pillar of Islam that my mum strictly adhered to was the difficult but humbling act of fasting. Unfortunately, when it became obligatory for me to fulfil this religious duty, the lunar Islamic calendar was displaying summer, and in my long ago youth, summers really were summers. Gloriously long, hot days tasted delicious during the school holidays as each drop of sunshine was absorbed with full appreciation of its ability to put smiles on people's faces; except when they were hungry: tired, lethargic, thirsty and hungry. Depriving the body of all its essential requirements from sunrise to sunset is a cruel experience, especially when that body is a mere twelve years old.

I lay sprawled across the carpet, light-headed and weak, staring intensely at the minute hand of the clock. Each second lasted a lifetime as I waited for it to strike ten. No food or water had entered my body for over seventeen hours and I was on the verge of collapse! My first ever-genuine full fast was drawing to an end. All day, my older siblings and I had fantasised about food. We would try to sleep during the day to help pass some of the long hours before sunset. As we lay in our beds, curtains drawn to block out the sunlight, our mouths dribbled with saliva. We visualised spicy samosas and melt in the mouth mangoes making their way towards our mouths. This self-torture would continue until we fell asleep in the bright sunlight, our bodies surrendering to the lure of semi-consciousness.

And at precisely ten o clock the binge would begin. We would break the fast with a date – a food that is considered healthy for the body and has a religious significance. With the date, I would recite a small prayer thanking God for the food before us. For a few seconds, I would feel genuine heartfelt appreciation for all the culinary delights in front of us, deciding that I would never be ungrateful or complain about anything ever again.

A huge, round tray filled with spicy savouries would be awaiting demolition. Those who weren't fasting had to show some self control as they did not deserve the food as much as the more pious amongst us. Slowly, each pakora, kebab, samosa and lamb chop would disappear. Only when the prime pickings were consumed did we move on to the more mundane foods: boring fruits such as apples and grapes and homemade poppadoms dipped in masala tea: you had to move quickly before the home-made poppadoms became too soggy to survive the journey from cup to mouth! The curry was a last resort if our appetites hadn't been satisfied. By the end of the feast, it became almost impossible to get up from the floor. Our bodies became heavy and lazy, and at the age of twelve, I was allowed to stay sprawled and useless on the floor, avoiding the necessary chore of clearing up after myself.

The next fast and the fast after that became less like a punishment and more of a spiritual undertaking. Year after year, one month of the year, I would make a humble attempt at walking in the shoes of the less fortunate: the poor, the vulnerable and the hungry. It was never close to the reality - how could it be? I had a guarantee of nourishment at the end of the day, unlike the millions with nothing but hope to keep their spirits alive. However, for a short few hours in the day, usually around lunchtime when the body expects food, I would feel weak, hungry and develop a very short temperament. My rumbling stomach would be screaming for something, anything to ease the turbulence within. Once it realised that there was nothing to be had, it quietly accepted its punishment, and the fast would become easier.

Chapter Fourteen

The real high school

My second year of high school began its journey in a larger place of intimidation and fear. Third, fourth and fifth years loomed over us, making us conscious of our every move. Castle Hill, the annexe was a mere introduction to the perils and dangers of a fully-fledged, bully bulging nightmare of a building.

At least the school bus run had lost the novelty of being the most terrifying experience of my life. Just like I had grown accustomed to my dad lashing out on my mum during moments of weakness and cowardice, so, I grew accustomed to insecure fellow pupils throwing unfounded insults and occasional saliva straight at me. It no longer worried me to walk on to a bus full of loud, ranting teenagers searching for their next victim, although the fear of the unknown, that sense that something could happen at any moment, was always a lingering threat that took many years to shake off.

Castle Mount High school had more than one floor. The corridors were colour coded to help the less confident to find their way round. Young, inexperienced faces wondered around, hopelessly lost and slightly panicked at the thought of asking for help in case they were re-directed in to a store cupboard. I had heard wild tales of new, naive faces being introduced involuntarily to the horrid insides of a toilet basin. Other dreaded delights included having your long plaits of hair, nurtured for several years, chopped off or perhaps a simple dissecting of your school tie would be your punishment for being in the right place at the right time with the wrong people.

There were more exclusive forms of torture for the less fortunate amongst us. A brown skin automatically granted you that privilege of exclusivity. Name-calling was absolutely the norm, and was to be expected around every corner and corridor around school. Daily insults such as 'Paki' and 'Nigger' were thrown at us with a deep conviction that somehow we would be upset or hurt by their foul language, but we could only laugh silently at the irony of their presumptuous convictions that they were somehow superior.

The insults were always incorrect, yet they were said with such pleasure and confidence by my fellow students that their sense of superiority allowed me to mock them secretly. I had enough self worth and enough sense to know that it was they who were worthy of insults, but because of my belief in my own convictions I had the faith to rise above it. The easiest thing in the world is to hide within a majority and tear out the limbs bit by bit of a minority. Fortunately, this member of the minority was strong enough to shield herself from the tormentors and interpret their insults as insecurities on their part that could only be healed through some positive life experiences. The embedded ideology of white supremacy that began its life several centuries ago was working its way through the high school culture at its mildest form, yet its presence was always there, knowingly or unknowingly.

In high school, we were placed into ability sets, which fortunately for me, meant that I was with my best friend Sameena for all the subjects. Razia was in the set below for most of the subjects, so the three of us gathered to chew the cud only at breaks and lunchtimes. Now it all seemed to get serious. The brighter students were gathered together to indulge in some serious learning, whilst the students considered to be 'slow learners' were set aside to help them achieve targets and goals that were set below their official age abilities. The segregation of society had begun: a necessary segregation to help the academically less able reach the expectations of the national average, and the gifted to thrive within a fast paced, challenging learning environment.

The scene had been set for the development of a mindset within a child, dictating their view of themselves and what they were capable of achieving. Those who found themselves in the lower sets were now labelled as underachievers. The hierarchical triangle that forms our modern society had already taken hold and embedded its roots at the tender age of eleven. Some of those roots break free and therefore break the expected trend of achievement, but many become entrenched deeper and deeper into what society expects from them. Being a teacher myself, I know how difficult it is to consider a fair, cheap alternative that would help to restore the self-esteem of the less able, and ensure the best progression of the gifted, which is probably why we continue to group children into ability sets today, labelling them and moulding their futures.

Enough of the politics; children can be extremely cruel. Victimisation was a common occurrence in schools but not all the victims were students. Some uninspiring teachers lay open targets for the pupils who had the fire and the balls to challenge them. There was no trace of fire in me. Such disrespect was unacceptable behaviour and I knew I would never participate in this cruelty – a sentiment shared by most of my fellow students. However, a handful of pupils more than made up for our angelic natures. Their outward behaviour provided an excellent form of entertainment for us all. Our Geography lesson was taught in a room far too small for thirty growing children, and having an extremely overweight teacher with sweat glands that often overexerted themselves, didn't help with the problem of lack of space. It was clear that he was self-conscious of his weight and this display of insecurity deflated his self -

confidence to the bare minimum.

Occasionally, I would feel sorry for him. He tried shouting over their voices, but this just made it worse as the crescendo of hackling and jeering overtook the voice that was meant to ooze authority and demand respect. A simple learning point..."and this is how chocolate is imported from Brazil"...would get a response from a loud-mouthed student at the back of the room of ..." is that what you had for your breakfast sir?" If the teacher was going to be let off the hook, a gentle hum of laughter would follow, and he would be allowed to continue 'teaching'. Sometimes however, the wolves were after more. The jeering would continue..."and for lunch, tea, dinner and a midnight feast!!" This would aggravate things even further, and eventually the instigator and his lackeys would be sent away to someone with more authority.

Two rooms down the corridor, another teacher won over the respect of virtually all his pupils by ensuring that he laid out the law the very first moment that we entered his domain. Once the law was laid down, he ensured that he carried out the promised punishments, and handed out the deserved rewards. Another skill that he possessed was the power to maintain our interest. We wanted to learn about the invasion of the Vikings because he made the era come alive. History gave him a genuine thrill and he was eager to pass his enthusiasm for the subject on to us: props and costumes, jumping enthusiastically on the tables, performing emotional role plays and involving all of us by incorporating our different strengths guaranteed a lively and willing learning environment.

Naturally, not every person in the room wanted to be there, but the difference between this room and the one down the corridor was glaringly obvious. Not wanting to learn was a choice that individuals made, but stalling the learning of others is a minor crime. Our history teacher did not allow the latter to happen and didn't particularly care for the individuals who made the choice to let themselves down by opting out from a privileged education system.

Chapter Fifteen

The return of the secret.

My secret 'lover' was back. He had escaped from my clutches when he moved away with his family in the last year of primary school, but I had heard on the grapevine that the only boy to have filled my heart with fluttering dreams and crazy notions of romance had returned to his true home, and to his true love!

Fantasyland has always been a happy place. In reality, I couldn't even share the same air or stand in the same room as him without my heart racing away from my body and my nerves shattering into a million pieces. These feelings scared me because they were in control of my thoughts and influenced simple decisions such as where I should sit at lunchtime or which route I should take when walking home.

One day, I crossed a busy road - for him. I only needed a little encouragement. It came in the form of Sameena. How incredibly silly and annoyingly girly I must have looked! Thinking about it now fills me with embarrassment. It was such a small incident, but yet so contradictory to my personality that the cringe-worthiness of the situation overwhelms me completely.

We must have walked for ten minutes on the opposite side of the road, him being completely unaware of my presence, and me, fantasising about how he wants to scream my name and walk with me hand in hand, never to be apart again! I experienced a moment of madness as I ran across the busy road just at the point where he couldn't miss me; a little look maybe? A momentary meeting of the eyes? The fleeting fantasy temporarily crumbled away as I remained invisible to him. But I felt no disappointment. At least I was now physically closer to him, enabling my fantasies to be even more intimate, maybe even feel more real as the distance between us closed in.

The following week I made breakfast for my fantasy: cornflakes and a cup of tea made by my own fair hands for my own Prince charming, and he knew that it was my hands that had sculpted what was in front of him. I had satisfied his hunger, calmed the rumblings. It was me. He also happened to be a friend of my older brother, but I chose to dismiss that fact, temporarily.

From a Western point of view, I was, and still am, an incredibly simple, unadventurous girl when it comes to investigating and exploring the male species. From an Islamic point of view, my modesty and respect when in male company is a positive attribute of my personality. My parents never laid down the law about boys when we were young teenagers, we were just supposed to know, and somehow, we did. I never had any desires to act upon my emotions in real life. Yes, I was scared of the consequences and realistically I was far too plain and ordinary next to him, but outside of my fantasy world, I didn't want to familiarise myself with boy creatures. It never sat comfortably with me and I knew that I would not be able to live with myself if some of those dream sequences playing in my head ever seeped in to my reality.

Yet it was part of life for some of my fellow Muslims. These so called 'misfits', who could dismiss the teachings of Islam, and embrace the Western culture so openly, became famous names within the community. My teenage years saw the first open rebellion of a generation against a religion and culture that discouraged any form of relationship with the opposite sex outside of marriage. Only a select few chose to be the instigators, but their determination and independence was the beginnings of a modern Muslim generation where pre-marriage relationships are commonplace.

Being a witness to these key developments in Anglo-Muslim behaviour was confusing and challenging. Firstly, how could it be so easy? I often wrongly jumped to the conclusion that they were 'bad' Muslims, and judged their behaviour to be a ticket that would take them straight in to hell. I was jealous of their freedom. They were not tied to the chains of guilt and decency which when younger, I interpreted as a negative. Yet I knew that I could never do what they were doing. I had neither the confidence nor the desire. However, simplifying this 'progression' into a simple equation of bad equals hell and good equals heaven, made everything less complicated to a young mind that wanted simple reasoning.

My conversations with boys were always for practical purposes and never for pleasure, yet there were a couple of Muslim girls in my year group who dared to indulge in flirty chats with the opposite sex. The eyelashes fluttered and the girly giggles grabbed attention. It was fascinating. They were fascinating. I wanted to experience being them, to embody all the emotions and thought processes that were alien to me, even if it wouldn't be for very long. My heart and soul would eventually reject these actions that contradicted everything that was true to me. But maybe in the short term I could soak up the attention and enjoy the temporary feelings of security that would do wonders for my self-esteem.

I heard rumours of couples. The words boyfriend and girlfriend stole in to my conversations instead of remaining some faraway images that only existed on the television: Couples - forming and breaking, everything happening in dark corners, in secret, away from adult eyes.

These young Muslims who chose to lie to their families for shared moments of intimacy puzzled me. They clouded my simple view on life. God was pleased with those who loved him by following His commandments. I wasn't even aware that temptations existed until my fellow Muslims began to dabble in them, and as time went on, the temptations gained speed, cowering over me, beckoning me to have a little taste. Eventually, many years down the line, I gave in to the cries for a brief period of time…

Chapter Sixteen

Home sweet home?

The troughs and peaks representing our home life continued to tease us with periods of calm and short bursts of terror. It didn't seem to matter that we had grown accustomed to the emotionally turbulent gorilla bouncing around our four, closed in walls...the pounding heart beat and quivering body never failed to rear its ugly head at the first sign of a potential beating targeted at my mum.

Picture this... two young teenagers and a woman looking much older than her years sat on a carpeted floor, legs crossed, pulling pieces of string that are attached to the walls. They remain in their positions for over two hours, even more at the weekends, almost every day for nearly ten years.

It was part of our daily lives; making Christmas crackers at home. After a few years of respite, my mum had resumed her home-based employment. Despite the seasonal demand, the manufacture of bangs and giggles continued throughout the year. It was in fashion, slave labour, all the neighbours were doing it and we were no exception. Frank the crackers man made his weekly trip to our sweatshop, taking the goods away, replacing them with fresh raw materials and handing over a wage packet that would have made the minimum wage of those days blush with embarrassment.

Hundreds of thousands of crackers were manufactured in my home. The essential tools were the hollow metal pipes: one long, one short. Put them together, get some fancy paper. Place snap (bang creator), incredibly funny joke and highly fashionable party hat in centre. Glue top lip of paper. Place pipes on all the aforementioned and roll. Wrap the string, which is tied to the nail in the skirting board, around the paper-covered pipes; make a gap between the long and small pipe and pull. The first strangulation is complete, and we have created one neck of the Christmas cracker. Repeat again, but remember to slide very exciting toy through pipe before strangulation with string. Pack into small, attractive boxes. Stick seasonal stickers on to front of each cracker. Job done.

It was tedious and tiring. Our legs remained tucked under ourselves for hours, and muscles in our back screamed for relaxation, but our young bodies were resilient. The pain would dissolve away five minutes after the shift, and for the rest of the day, we would forget about the work that still needed to be done. For that, there was always tomorrow.

And so, year upon year, we continued with our child labour. Not that it ever felt like we were being used or abused by our mum. She had no alternative, and she never forced us to work, it was a necessity that was never questioned. Even at such a tender age, the harsh realities of life were clear to us. Since our birth, we never experienced a steady stream of happiness and innocent laughter, and so, we never expected it.

Chapter Seventeen

Moving home

It was time for us to relocate. Unfortunately, we were not promoting ourselves away from the terraced jungle in to the land of the semi-detached: it was a stone's throw away to another line of deteriorating terraces in urgent need of repair. After my dad had successfully renovated our corner terrace into a three bed-roomed modern home many years ago, it seemed our imminent move wasn't a sly step sideways, but a demeaning demotion back to the world of slug trails and mouse droppings.... my dad was yet again failing. He was unable to keep up the increased mortgage repayments and the consequence of his neglect was a big step back to living in a home that was in the same state as our failing family unit.

Our teenage years dictated the need for separate sibling bedrooms but our new, decrepit home provided only two, and so my parents replaced their sleeping quarters with the bed settees in the living room. The back of the settees would fold back flat, and once layered with a couple of heavy Indian duvets, they would make the most comfortable of beds.

The physical state of our home spoke as a metaphor for the state of our family. I recall only darkness in that house,

113

darkness and loneliness. The freedom of playground streets and easy friendships seemed to have escaped this part of the terraced jungle: memories of slug trails and cockroaches had always been diminished by stronger memories of long summer days and a genuine feeling of love despite the many hurdles. But when I try and recall the emotions that enveloped this part of my life, sadness and a sense of nothing dominates.

My dad's gambling was exceeding beyond control, and the bad moods were becoming vicious. There was no sense of self-control and respect in our home as the month of Ramadan approached. Inner peace and tranquillity were the ultimate targets during this sacred month, but instead, we remained constantly on edge.

The breaking of the fast was not a family occasion, as my dad would either be in bed, or out performing wrongful acts, rather than acts of worship. And on his return, whatever time of day or night, we would be on watch duty, guarding our mum from potential beatings, or verbal abuse for simply being herself.

The climax of the holy month of Ramadan came when all except the pious Muslims of the British population were tucked safely in bed. We had reluctantly left our warm cocoons of the working man's silk to observe the prayer and taking of food before sunrise. It seemed so cruel to have to take ourselves away from this haven that allowed us to indulge in sub-conscious happiness. Dreams that promised a certainty that real life never did.

Our mum yelled from the bottom of the stairs. Naturally, we ignored her initial wake up calls, somehow hoping she would give up and let us go back to our haven of peaceful dreams. But her persistence remained and eventually it became easier to give in rather than maintain tranquil in our cocoons. Eyes half open, hair dishevelled and mind in limbo, we made our way down to disturb the nocturnal creatures that inhabited our home during the night. The slugs raced back at their own pace into the crevices by which they made their entrance. Mice scurried away as the human disturbance interrupted their search for a night-time feast. It was our turn to feast, although in the middle of the night the task of consuming a fiery curry seemed impossible. Instead, a bland piece of toast made soggy by a dip into a cup of tea seemed more realistic. It was necessary to fill the belly before sunrise to help maintain our energy throughout the fast. It was also necessary to say the prayer after sunrise to ensure the intentions of the fast were sincere although it was too easy to bypass this act of worship, as the lure of the warm cocoon upstairs was far more welcoming.

One night during that month of Ramadan, as we staggered down the stairs in our usual comatose state, we stepped in to a strange atmosphere; an atmosphere that posed a serious threat but unusually, without the threat of violence. Instead, there was an eerie stillness. My mum was keeping quiet without the help of her children. There was no pressing urgency to remove her from the room. My dad was also calm. There was a look of despair about him, and a reluctance to say whatever was on his mind. Just as we prepared for whatever the moment promised to bring, a loud bang reverberated in the street and through the terraced walls. The stillness should have been replaced by panic and curiosity, but instead the eeriness held its ground. Only my big brother was moved by the commotion outside and decided to investigate.

A full-scale drama was unfolding in the street. A joy rider had crashed his illegally driven car in to another car and as most of the residents in the street were awake, the police had been alerted and crowds were gathering. It was unusual for the residents to be provided with such riveting entertainment in the middle of the night and to be awake for it!

My brother was thoroughly enjoying the free live show and was not too pleased when I had to call for him to hurry back into our own, less thrilling and far more serious slice of life. The scene in our reality show was slowly revealing itself, and the words my dad was uttering were so familiar. I had heard such words many times on the television, in soap operas and documentaries, but they were not supposed to be uttered in my reality.

He let the words out reluctantly; who do you want to live with, mum or me? A simple question. The answer seemed simple and obvious too. None of us would choose to live with our dad. He was unpredictable: an adult figure that promised only insecurities and mistrust. On the other hand, my mum, despite her insecurities within herself, was a solid figure of reliability. She had never let us down and never would let us down. My simple, immature mind quickly said aloud what we were all thinking. Mum. We wanted to live with mum.

As soon as the words left my mouth, my older siblings hushed me. At the age of thirteen everything was straightforward. I was being given a choice of living life without the fear of my mum being oppressed emotionally and physically. I would no longer have to bear witness to the pain my mum went through every day of her life. But it seems that life wasn't that simple, and even though my siblings were only a couple of years older than me, they had managed to work out how the system worked. Together was better, despite the pain. It seemed that we needed both our parents and they both needed each other. So I was told to be quiet. Silence was to be our response to the unwanted question.

The moment passed. My dad got his answer. We were doomed to share the future, whatever it might bring.

Quietly, we consumed our soggy toast and slid back into our cocoons. Those of us who were old enough to understand what had just happened indulged in our private thoughts: we reflected on the possibilities and outcomes, and soon the incident became just another episode of pain that fell from our young memories in to a cauldron of what seemed like normality.

The year of misery passed by. Time quickly healed the wounds of that dramatic night and as children, we let the experience escape from our minds. We were moving on again. Time had also healed the debts and troubles of a gambling dad and it was yet another fond farewell to the pests and creatures that shared our habitat.

We moved yet again to another line of terraces just a stone's throw away from the last one. The house we moved into was due for a government grant and the house next door was occupied by an old lady who was rumoured to be considering a quick sale in the very near future. My forward-thinking dad had already planned to buy the house next door and use the government grant to join the two terraces in to one large family home. Clever; Asian clever!

For now, we still occupied a house that was too small for a family of seven. The bathroom was built into our bedroom, and the box-room was given to my brothers leaving my parents to double up the living room as a bedroom. However, this house felt much cleaner, and the future was also promising to be brighter, and so, we continued working hard, both at home and at school, and waited for OUR mansion to magically arise from the ground.

Sometimes, home did feel like sweet home: when we watched Bollywood movies in our little living room, in the dark, munching on home-made popcorn; there was the option of salted or chilli popcorn, with a little turmeric added in the oil to give it that authentic Indian look. My dad was always part of our happy family, as he was the one who would go to the shop to rent the video for the night, and found them thoroughly entertaining.

Ignorance is no excuse, but at the innocent age of thirteen, I found the predictable, nauseating plots of the Bollywood movie thoroughly entertaining too! Just like the authentic Indian audience back home, we were mesmerised by the colours, sounds and far-fetched love stories that dominated the genre. The music temporarily whisked us away to a pleasant, flower filled world where wooing your lover with romantic lyrics and ridiculous dances was perfectly sane.

On one occasion, I found myself quietly weeping whilst watching a highly emotional scene. The room was dark in the hope of creating a cinematic effect, and I was hoping that my tears would pass by un-noticed; however, when you are surrounded by four siblings who are looking for every opportunity to make a mockery out of you, such teasing potential is never wasted.

They sneered at my incapability to hold back my emotions. They laughed and called me a baby for crying over something that wasn't even real, but my dad jumped to my defence. I was the only one who cried, because I was the only one who truly understood the story line. It was only I who had the intelligence to truly appreciate the heart rendering conversation between the two characters, and so, could not control my tears. His words made me smile because I was sharing one of those rare moments with him where he made me feel special: some positive attention that did wonders for my self-esteem.

Chapter Eighteen

The Two Intellects

High school was now routine. Our teenage years were rolling by and our personalities were developing concepts and beliefs that were never swayed or influenced by peer pressure. Sameena and I considered ourselves different from our peers. We considered ourselves to have a liking for the sort of conversations that seemed beyond the reach of most of our friends. Our evidence for this highly pompous presumption was the fact that we were never able to have a conversation with our peers that was even close to the conversations we had with each other. Even at that young age we were not naïve enough to think that our thirst for grown up talk somehow made us superior to our peers – it was a mere observation and an indication of the choices we would make in the future.

Our conversations ranged from idle gossip to putting the world to rights. We would discuss the latest rebel, acting against religious teachings and against their parent's wishes. The secret meetings that enabled such proceedings to be enacted required meticulous planning and inevitably led to an intricate web of deceit and lies. Our lack of experience with reality led us to conclude that such rebellious behaviour was a result of immorality and an absence of parental guidance. We were blind to the possibility that they were simply answering the natural desire and curiosity to explore the opposite sex. That side of our own desires hadn't yet surfaced and we were quick to judge others without understanding that taking the moral high ground was in itself a misguidance.

Many conversations also led to our fantastical view of our futures. Most of these fantasies involved a fusion of both the western ideals of modern life and the deep-rooted Islamic concept of religion as the way of life. Our favourite fantasy was the one involving a lush city apartment; our very own independent pad where we would have complete freedom to choose what to do with our lives and how to live that life. Our personalities would be splattered all over the walls with our impeccable taste in interior design and we would live a life where our thoughts and desires were carefully considered and processed before they were acted upon.

Then there was the fantasy of the millionaire who would declare his undying love and sweep us off our feet. Not an exclusive fantasy but unfortunately a very exclusive reality. Hearts would flutter and minds wander as we had long, whole hearted discussions outlining in detail how we would meet this self-made millionaire who had all the personality of a Hollywood hero with the morals and beliefs of a pious Muslim. The superhero himself was a paradox as the two ideals had contradictory life styles that were in reality on the opposite ends of the scale. How could the jeans and leather clad hero, with the deep swooning eyes and chiselled face ever resemble the juba wearing, long bearded Muslim? Yet many of our fantasies about the ideal men resembled a fusion of east and west – it seems our imaginations were also confusing the two cultures that dominated our lives.

'Those who find themselves religious...sit down next to me'...Song lyrics that suggested that religion can cause emotional and spiritual turmoil within a person yet it would be impossible for him to live without it. When I heard those lyrics for the first time, I felt uneasy. Religion had never left me confused before and I presumed that all those lucky enough to be religious shared that sentiment, however, as the reality of growing up and the many emotions and desires that it brings with it began stirring within me, I realised that the reality away from the terraced jungle was far more challenging and thought provoking than I could have ever imagined.

One of those confusing desires was my secret love: unrequited and fantastical, but thoughts of him tapped into feelings that were otherwise untouched. In private, I was convinced that our destinies were matched and our futures belonged together.

In the real world, where my dream man didn't even

know I existed, life went on. I wasn't pining over him – my well balanced brain instructed me that that would be futile, but the odd dabble in some pointless pondering of what if's and fantasies gave me a moment of something I wasn't to experience for a long time to come.

I was a conformist. The people around me were all conformists in one-way or another. Culture was a factor in conformity. The community accepted their way of life instead of challenging themselves to change for the better. That is contradictory to the laws of Islam that state that one must strive to improve one's life in this world within the laws of the religion and then accept the outcome as God's decision.

Awf ibne-Malik r.a narrates that the prophet Muhammed, peace be upon him, gave a decision between two men. And that the one against whom the decision had been given, turned away and said :(Allah is sufficient for me and what an excellent Disposer of affairs is He). Thereupon the prophet Muhammed, peace be upon him, remarked: Allah T'ala condemns inadequate efforts. Therefore, carry out your affairs diligently and intelligently. However in spite of this, if a matter overpowers you then say: (Allah is sufficient for me and what an excellent Disposer of Affairs is He).

(Muntakhab ahadith. Organised and presented by Hazart Maulana Muhammad Sa'ad Kandhlawi)

The dominant blind faith element of the community, as well as culture and tradition, dictated that the women must stay at home and remain subservient to the men. Female psyche was such that they believed their lives would be reduced to shame and humiliation without a man to dominate over them. My dad was the negative product of this world where he conformed to society's expectations. My mum had this concept of the female embedded within her since childhood. Her circumstances were the product of an Indian culture not of the Islamic faith. She unwittingly sacrificed her own happiness for her children: a noble gesture. Today, many would consider this gesture as stupidity, asking the question - how can the children be happy living in such a destructive environment? But each home experiences different levels of suffering and are not always presented with a better alternative. Because of my mum's complete lack in confidence and ignorance of how the western world worked, she would have been lost and helpless without her intact family unit. The idea of shattering the only life she had ever known would have destroyed her own sense of self.

We all conform to what we know and feel comfortable with. Those of us who are unable to conform either become disillusioned and disappointed with life, or we become incredible success stories, inspiring others and living our life to its fullest whether that be a materialistic achievement or a spiritual one.

As a true conformist, I blended in to the background as much as my skin colour would allow me. My inherited capacity to produce good results in exams gave me the opportunity to brush shoulders with the elite of the school. I had the opportunity to socialise with like-for-like peers. These students were blissfully unaware of the colour of my skin or my skinny trousers. They looked past the fact that my hair looked the same every single day and respected me for having my own personality, views and moods.

School, moods and views continued to change and develop as my early teenage years built their store of memories. My last couple of years at high school involved many more intellectual conversations that filled our heads with an assumed opinion that we were different when compared with our fellow Muslim peers. Our peers also assumed that we were different. Our lack of interest in their day-to-day lives suggested bland personalities, and although we weren't disliked, our position on the popularity scale was hovering just below the average.

Chapter Nineteen

Finding my form in the sixth form

G.C.S.E's done: revision consisted of two weeks of intense cramming that seemed to suffice. I achieved good grades. Not genius grades but enough to enter in to the sixth form. Our French teacher 'assisted' us by using her thumb to indicate the past, present or future tense during our oral tests. This subtle guidance played a part in helping me to achieve an unexpected B in the subject.

The expected build up of nerves and pressure that many students experience before sitting an exam surpassed my psyche. Although my parents were aware that I was about to take some potentially life-changing exams, there was no pressure from them to achieve top grades. This however, was not neglect or a lack of interest on their part. It was the result of living lives that were wrapped around a demanding culture of freshly made curries, extended family feuds and menacing mood swings that overshadowed the importance of their children's education.

Sixth form demanded maturity. We were there by choice and so, were expected to be model students: easily achieved by the straight-laced me. My older sister had chosen to study Economics and Maths so it was only natural that I should follow in her footsteps. It was the safe thing to do. I did however manage to make one independent choice by also opting for an A level in English. Entertainment through words stimulated my mind: exploring hidden meanings and asserting my creativity through words gave me pleasure. It was the subject that was going to influence my choices in my later educational life, but it was the teacher of my Economics class that was influencing my thoughts at that moment in time!

Slightly below-average looking; old; receding hairline and lanky; but Mr Evans was the starring role in my newfound fantasies. Something was changing inside me: maturity of the mind? Sexual awakening? Call it what you will, but I sensed a definite change. It wasn't just butterflies in my stomach, it wasn't just the odd fantasy – I felt something stir inside me; an indefinable something that demanded my attention. My newly found, slightly perverted obsession arose from the unfounded rumour that Mr Evan's wife was dying of cancer. This sad news instantly fired up my nurturing instincts. I wanted to hold him in my arms and tell him everything was going to be fine. Those puppy eyes seemed to be asking me for exactly that as I interpreted the explanation of the theory of supply and demand as a call for emotional support! Many an hour I stared into those eyes imagining my arms wrapped around his lean waist as he continued to share his knowledge of Mr Faraday to those of us who cared to listen.

His geeky sticky out ears are still etched deep in to my thoughts of the past. The bulbous nose and balding head remain firmly rooted in my distorted memory and clearly had a lasting impact on my teenage fantasies. I'd like to consider it perfectly normal for a teenager to have a crush on their teacher, but a rather strange looking one, facing the possibility of a dying wife, would have to be considered slightly perverse!

With sixth form came the beginnings of social divide. I was now with my peers: like for like people who all had enough brain capacity to attempt the demanding 'A' level. Intellectually, I was at ease with my environment. Conversations were mature - not frilly and frustrating. The subject of boys (and balding men!) always gave way to giddy behaviour, but apart from this distraction, I was in my element.

I took for granted the luxury of owning my time. Every second of the day was devoted to my own selfish needs. Pressure only reared its ugly head when deadlines threatened to fail my assignments or exams loomed, but these pressures were insignificant compared to the strains and demands of real life that were lying in waiting.

Our friendship circle expanded as Sameena and I discovered other Muslim girls that were closer to our snobbish intellect than we ever thought possible! Girls from different backgrounds that provided us with the knowledge that some Asian families were in fact 'normal' and consisted of stable, solid environments where the children were sheltered from any negativity or pain. It seemed that every other child did not have to put up with that gorilla bouncing off the walls.

Subconsciously, our friendship choices always steered towards female Muslims; much like a Goth, who would be drawn to a fellow Goth because of their familiar exterior and the likelihood of matching personalities. In high school, we were often met with disappointment, but in this funnelled social environment the odds were favouring us.

By the end of the first year we had formed our own clique: A handful of young women who shared similar viewpoints and also shared a mutual confidence that our lives were moving in the right direction. The verbal abuse and physical taunts that were so commonplace at high school were less frequent. This encouraged our personalities to develop without the hindrance of our insecurities surfacing. It was a return back to my childhood days when I felt protected by the close community and at this stage in my life it was my own self-belief that was protecting me from the distorted views of the wider world.

One of our most entertaining and educational lessons was pure maths. It wasn't the mathematical elements of the lesson that sourced the amusing way of passing time but the to and fro of notes that passed between Sameena and me. Mr Tate was a timid, uninspiring teacher, who taught his subject with the assumption that his audience were already captivated by logarithms and hyperbolic functions! A minority of the students did have an incredible talent and enthusiasm for the mathematical linguistics, however, this was not a watered down version of maths and its purity confounded me.

And so, trying to understand how our teenage, hormonal minds worked seemed to be a much more interesting and entertaining option. Mr Tate was suspicious of our alternative curriculum; however, he seemed to be turning a blind eye to it - probably because he had already predicted the near fail grades that we were to achieve at the end of the academic year.

Our supply of sticky notes and note pads was carefully maintained as we asked each other questions about our past, present and future. We shared our innermost feelings and desires and explored each other's thoughts on the people and places around us. Our language was usually polite and considerate, with words that expressed our opinions succinctly. Passionate, fiery temperaments were foreign to us and our words reflected this with an absence of abuse and profanities. We were at our happiest when sharing our intimate thoughts and sometimes distorted views, whatever the means to achieving this was.

Chapter Twenty

Back to my roots

At the end of the first year of sixth form we embarked on our first family trip to India. My little brother had been abroad at a very young age with our mum, but this was the first time that we were to have a real family holiday away from the temperamental British summer. Our culture hadn't yet bought in to the idea of visiting countries other than India – understandably, my parents and many like them, only considered using their hard earned cash to go back home and see their families and revisit the lives that they had reluctantly left behind so many years ago.

The flight fare was not wasted. We were to spend our whole summer holiday in India – making the most of the sweat and tears it took to raise the money for the fare in the first place. Although excited about the concept of going abroad, we remained sceptical as to whether it would feel like a real holiday – whether we would be escaping from the one thing that was still consistent in our lives – the unpredictable moods of my dad.

With five children in tow, from the oldest of 19 to the youngest of 10, it wasn't going to be an easy flight. We were also somewhat neglecting our duties as the domestic abuse police as the excitement of boarding a plane overtook our usual precautionary status when in the company of our parents. We were both excited and flustered as we looked for our seats amongst the babble of people. After a little confusion, we managed to find our row and were quibbling about who was to sit where, when my dad grabbed mine and my sister's plaits from behind us and physically pulled us down on to our seats. The tug was sharp and sudden. He was clearly annoyed with all the fuss we were making and instead of recognising that it was our excitement and innocence that caused us to quibble, he became impatient and angry at our seemingly lack of ability to organise our selves quickly and efficiently.

I sensed people looking at us. It was a strange feeling, as my dad's abuse up till now had remained within four walls and displayed only in front of family members. Now, there were perfect strangers all around me who were making a judgement about my dad and about our reaction to it. We remained silent for a while as my parents sat behind us, waiting for the moment to pass.

The next burst of anger came when the immigration forms had to be completed before entry in to Bombay airport. My dad had seven pieces of paper all requiring information and in truly Asian style, he presumed that it had to be done as quickly as possible to avoid queues and ensure that we were dealt with efficiently. We wanted to help him, but were anxious that our interference might not be appreciated and therefore tried to stay out of his way. However, my dad's frustrations were building up as he watched his useless children again displaying a lack of initiative by not helping him with the simple task of completing a few forms. As he filled in the last one, he expressed his disgust for us by offering some profanities and a few choice words of advice as to how we should make ourselves more useful.

Eventually, the escape route from the stifling heat of the oppressive air that seemed to be lingering in every nook and cranny of the airport came to view. There was a real smell of corruption and the sense that we were no longer in control. My dad's demeanour was one of apprehension as we waited in the passport control queue. He smiled at us nervously, telling us to stop wearing such miserable faces without any trace of conviction in his voice. The next queue involved the inspection of our luggage – including a brand new TV that my dad decided to bring with him. It was the perfect excuse for the corrupt airport officers to extort some money out of my dad. They seized the television, claiming that such baggage was illegal and called my dad to one of their back offices to 'negotiate'. After a few hundred pounds of negotiation, the television was released – the television that had now doubled its purchase price!

The doors swung open – our escape route from the overwhelming humidity and oppressive atmosphere had finally arrived. My naïve teenage mind was setting itself up for a happy holiday brochure welcome but what greeted us couldn't have been further away from the fake images they portrayed.

Instantly, we were attacked by hot oven baked heat: A heat that I had never experienced before. The humidity was even more oppressive than the inside of the airport. Rays of intense sun weakened my already tired body and my sense of smell was treated to an array of foreign stenches and aromas that my body battled to reject. Voices were yelling, talking and whispering all around me. We were told to walk quickly and keep hold of our luggage. Eye contact was to be avoided at all costs as a simple look would suggest that we required help to move our luggage. Men with sweaty, draping moustaches and tired, red eyes stared at us. There were hundreds of them gawping at the parade of passengers. We were apparently looking for our Indian relatives who had come to pick us up, but amongst the chaos of sounds and sights, it was difficult to spot the few people that I presumed would be 'civilised' compared to the rest of the crowd.

As we pushed our way through the sweaty bodies we spotted a small crowd of people waving furiously to get our attention…it was time to meet my Indian family – the family that till now were faces on photographs and names that were thrown about during family disagreements.

Three of my dad's siblings were permanently settled in England and three Indian uncles still remained in their home country with their families. A couple of my Indian cousins had come to greet us together with their fathers. It only took a few minutes of awkward conversation for me to realise that it was going to be difficult to connect to these people. My snobbery quickly took over the need for compromise and acceptance. I had judged the people in front of me in a matter of minutes and my immaturity and inexperience of life assured that this snobbery remained for the rest of the holiday.

My dad's village was a few hours train ride away. We waited for our luggage to be packed in to the infamous Indian Maruti people carrier that was to take us to the train station. As we stood impatiently in the searing heat the tame Indian flies unashamedly made themselves comfortable on our exposed feet. Thinking back to our reaction fills me with embarrassment but at the time we reacted to the flies on our feet by jumping up and down and squealing. The Indians must have considered our behaviour bizarre but at the time the numerous, fearless flies genuinely upset us.

We were packed into the van and within a few seconds I felt the heavenly cool air of the air conditioning hit my face. The joy lasted for just a few minutes until I opened my eyes to the reality of the world I had just entered and the world of privileges I had left behind at home.

The pavements were lined with makeshift homes constructed with everything from corrugated iron sheets to flimsy bin liners. Shop walls provided the support to keep them upright but the rest of their homes consisted of temporary constructions that provided them with a small public space they could call their own. Whilst driving past, I saw people brushing their teeth and washing their hair at the front of the public pavements. A bucket provided them with their bath water courtesy of the local businesses. The homes averaged the size of a standard box room, leaving little space for personal possessions and, as they were exposed to the outside world and the natural elements, it would have been futile to fill their homes with anything other than the basics needed for living.

We were stunned in to silence because of what we were witnessing. My dad had opened the windows to allow us to truly appreciate the hustle and bustle around us. The traffic was chaotic and beeping one's horn was the only method of communication on the roads. Traffic signals in the Bombay of 1991 were scarce and the driving population ignored them anyway. The traffic had its own unique system of utter chaos and it was yet another aspect of India that alienated me from my parent's home country.

Vehicles were not the only objects causing organised chaos on the roads. Cows are considered sacred in the

Hindu culture as they are seen as surrogate mothers who provide milk to human beings for the whole of their lives, as well as curd and butter. They are considered a great gift from mother-nature and are therefore left roaming freely amongst the traffic. Occasionally, a cow may decide to take a break by sitting itself down in the middle of the road, however, the revered respect given to cows means that no one mishandles it and so the traffic has to work its way around it!

The general public were also just as hazardous. They would bang the bonnets of cars to signal that they were crossing the road and that the vehicle, that was often just a few inches away from them, had to slow down! The whole system was fascinating to observe but yet again, my teenage mind was quick to judge the country as inferior and out of control compared to the tranquillity and order that England insisted upon.

Amongst the traffic roamed numerous beggars. Women with tiny babies targeted stand-still traffic. They outstretched their arms and cupped their hands, reaching in to people's open windows and gesturing at their hungry babies. Young children walked around with withering flowers, desperately attempting to sell them for a few rupees. Men with severed limbs and people without eyesight wandered the roads, dodging the traffic and staring into vehicles, hoping to win over somebody's pity.

The evidence of desperate poverty was all around me. People were scattered around the city, sleeping under bridges and on the edge of buildings trying to grab a siesta from the hot sun. And in and amongst this poverty were the official citizens of Bombay, the ones who were recognised as working; rent paying members of the public. Although these people had houses to live in, most of them were single room homes occupied by several members of the family. Some of them were inhabitants of shantytowns, whilst others paid extortionate amounts of rent for a single room above a shop or in a decrepit apartment or flat.

In the background, away from the bustle of the city and towering over the shantytowns, were the high-rise apartments and hotels that were occupied by the rich. Distribution of wealth was blatantly uneven and it was clear from the highly disproportionate percentage of the population that occupied the shantytowns and streets that movement up the social ladder was a near impossibility.

After an hour of trudging through the Bombay roads we eventually arrived at the train station. The Victorian building, built by the British and a pride of India, impressed my limited experience of grand architecture. Our tickets and luggage were organised by our uncles and we were soon boarding the train. We were spared from the real Indian train experience as my dad had instructed his brothers to book two first class carriages. It was a welcome break after the shock of seeing the real India. Although the view from the window during station stops still brought with them beggars and sellers, the air-conditioned carriage was strictly off limits for them. We enjoyed the views and relaxed for the first time since leaving what we now considered the luxuries of an economy class flight.

To a mature, inquisitive adult, the sights and sounds of a new country and new culture would have been a privilege: anything different from their own identity would bring out an enthusiasm and a natural curiosity to learn more. However, as a teenager, my interpretation of this backward, unhygienic culture was misguided. The people seemed desperate and ill mannered and their country was inconsiderate towards its visitors with its lack of order. The stench of the open sewage system offended my sense of smell. I was clearly suffering from a superiority complex as I considered my England much more advanced than this backward country: England offered a far more acceptable standard of living for all of its population compared to this world of mass poverty.

Within a few hours we had reached Bharuch railway station. Bharuch was the town closest to our village, Dayadra. Night had ascended upon us and the heat and the flies were allowing us some respite. Outside the station we boarded yet another Maruti van that was to take us to our home for the next six weeks.

The constant beeping on the busy roads was less frequent, although we still felt a sense of danger as trucks and motorbikes sped past with only a few inches between us. Abandoned vehicle wreckages on the side of the road told of the many disasters that resulted from the indiscriminate method of driving that had been adopted by the Indian road users. The roads were lined with trees and the lower parts of the trunks were painted with white, neon paint: when the headlights of the vehicles hit the paint they reflected a considerable amount of light, producing a cheap alternative to road lamps. The makeshift lights came to an end as we turned left into Dayadra.

Despite our late arrival, the village was still bustling with men. They were hanging out in what was the centre of the village, drinking glasses of Indian tea and chewing tobacco. Women and their families were gathered outside doorsteps, sharing conversations with neighbours amidst wandering goats and chickens. Our Maruti van drove through the village and made its first stop outside my oldest, late uncle's house, which was a traditional Indian village home. It was small, simple and its building materials partially consisted of cowpats!

My two sisters and me were taken on the first floor and asked to sit on the bed. Within minutes of sitting down, the room had filled up with the local female villagers. They all sat cross-legged on the floor and stared at the three of us.

Our arrival it seemed was big news, and the women had come to take a good look at us. They whispered and quietly giggled as we tried to get over the shock of being treated like animals at the zoo! Strangers, who were now introduced as my aunties, uncles and cousins, came to greet us. We smiled and shook their hands politely whilst feeling lost and confused in an alien environment. Again, we interpreted their behaviour as rude and inconsiderate. After hours of travelling, the British thing to do would be to show us to our rooms and allow us to rest for the night, leaving introductions to the next day, but the Indian hospitality that we were experiencing sharply contradicted this concept.

After around an hour of being viewed by starry-eyed women who considered our presence in their village a huge novelty, we piled back into the Maruti van. Within a few minutes we stopped outside the house that my other two uncles and my grandparents lived in – the house that my dad had worked so hard to pay for. Compared to our house back home, it appeared to be much bigger. The front porch was large enough to hold an adult swing that could take at least three adults at a time. There were several large windows on the ground floor that suggested that there were plenty of rooms downstairs and just as many upstairs. Bricks and mortar made the house appear ultra modern compared to the houses in the rest of the village and the tiled floor of the porch was glimmering, ready for its foreign visitors.

Finally, we were shown to our beds. In a matter of minutes the five of us were fast asleep, no longer aware of the unfamiliar environment we were sharing with our Indian family and with an Indian population that seemed a world away from our reality of cleanliness and etiquettes.

The next day we woke up to the sound of a crowing cockerel. It was our first look at the village in daylight and despite the early hours of the morning we were eager to explore. Still dressed in our pyjamas, we made our way downstairs to find a fully prepared Indian breakfast: purees and chilli omelette with masala tea. Although our taste buds were more familiar with beans on toast, we quickly obliged. Our hunger pangs were too strong to ignore.

After a quick inspection of the toilet facilities, which thankfully my dad had specified to be of the English variety, we got dressed and stepped out in to the hot sun to satisfy our curiosity.

The monsoon season had arrived in India but as yet there had been no downpours ensuring that our route through the village was free of squelching mud and out of control cowpats. We walked through the narrow streets, busy courtyards and dusty patches of dry grass drawing attention to ourselves simply by being British. The heat and humidity in the air was incredible and despite our attempts at dodging the stray dogs and bleating goats with grace we inadvertently provided the locals with a dose of comical entertainment.

Even amongst the relative poverty of the village there were reminders for the locals that they were living comfortable lives compared to some of their fellow residents. On the outskirts of the village lived the 'untouchables' – the lowest members of the Hindu caste system. Just like in Bombay, they used the strong wall of a house as their main support for their otherwise makeshift homes. There is no caste system in Islam so the Muslim community did accept their presence; however, society conceived the 'untouchables' worthy only of menial jobs. Their employment was limited to hard labour with wages that often only consisted of their daily ration of food.

After taking in the sights, sounds and smells of the village we returned back to the house. We spent the rest of the day getting to know our extended family and observing their daily routines. As evening approached, the skies darkened. The first monsoon rains were making their way towards the village. It was a much-anticipated moment for the villagers as they waited impatiently for the rains to come.

The darkness came and after a roar of thunder the skies opened up. It came down hard and fast, filling up the uneven surface of the ground with pools of water. Within the space of half an hour the village was transformed: crickets sang their songs and frogs croaked with utter glee; a damp smell filled the air and worst of all for us British, the moths came out in their thousands!

A long tube light was fixed on to one of the walls in the room where we were sitting. In a matter of minutes the whole illuminated wall was covered with moths and other tiny but terrifying creatures. Not an inch of wall space remained as they clambered over each other to get to the bright tube light. We could read the fear in each other's faces – and so could our parents. They escorted us in to the next, darkened room, where we remained till it was time to go to bed. After over twenty years, I still recall the image of the moth filled wall and the fear that overtook our young, inexperienced minds.

As the days passed by we grew accustomed to the fact that the creatures were part and parcel of the Indian experience. One night, my older brother made the mistake of leaving a peanut in his pyjama pocket. In the morning, as he slid his hand in, he pulled out a ball of ants that had set to work breaking up and transporting the peanut back to their nest. Small lizards lived in quiet corners of the ceiling, occasionally scurrying across the walls that often resulted in us also scurrying in to another room. Our eyes were on constant watch for the sudden movements of such harmless yet powerful creatures that were invisible to the native

Indian eye.

Mosquitoes also made their presence known. Despite taking all the necessary precautions, they could not resist the temptation of fresh, foreign blood. Lying on my side one night, I woke up the next morning with one half of my face and just one of my arms and legs covered with bites. The sight was amusing for others but humiliating and painful for me.

My parents were immune to the perils of insect life. My mum, however, demonstrated her phobia of frogs on one especially wet evening when the ditch outside the house was so full of rainwater that it had formed a miniature lake. The number of frogs was unusually high and some of them overflowed on to the porch, croaking and jumping around our feet regardless of the consequences. As soon as my mum realised that the wet creatures were near her, she screamed and quickly made her way indoors. Her behaviour seemed so unnatural as we had made the presumption that Indians were not supposed to fear the things that we, the British, feared. She remained indoors for the rest of the evening, refusing to share the same space as the noisy, inconsiderate beasts!

Every evening we went to different homes as guests for dinner. We craved our English meals as night after night we were subjected to traditional Indian cooking. The hosts of each home were overwhelmingly polite and forthcoming with their offerings of food however; we must have come across as incredibly ungrateful as we played with the food on our plates, unable to enjoy what the hosts considered their very best cuisine.

My dad allowed a couple of weeks to pass by to ensure that we had acclimatised to the country then he announced that we were to climb in to yet another Maruti van and go sightseeing for a couple of weeks. It was welcomed news as the days were beginning to fall in to a routine and the sense of being on holiday was diminishing.

The next day we packed our bags with pyjamas and a few pairs of clothes and we were off. As we started filling up the van, I noticed that it wasn't just our family that were to experience the jewels of India: it seemed that the maruti was going to be used to its full capacity as an auntie and an uncle and a cousin or two also joined our party of tourists.

As we left, driving through the village we heard someone screaming behind us. He was shouting for us to stop. The breathless boy was yet another cousin who wanted to join us. We stopped and he was allowed to come on board. His desperate fear of being left behind didn't leave any time for him to wear his own shoes so he stepped on to the van with his dad's size 10 slippers on and squeezed himself between us. By now, we were filled to well over capacity but this was of no significance in a country where road safety was a blind part of the law.

My parent's home was in the south of Gujarat and we were heading north towards Ahmadabad. Next we were to head further north into the state of Rajasthan enjoying its beautiful royal palaces and taking in the red city of Jaipur and finally in to Uttar Pradesh where we were to visit the iconic Taj Mahal in Agra. We were to take a round trip of over one thousand miles with many of the roads bumpy and treacherous. The tightly packed travelling conditions only added to the discomfort as we drove past other vehicles with only inches between us. The mountainous roads were especially frightening as we hung literally inches away from the edge. There was plenty of evidence displaying the horrific results of such a hazardous environment but it seemed that everyone around us was oblivious to it, including my officially British parents!

During our stops we stayed at what I would now consider basic hotels. Most of them had relatively clean toilets and were void of any nasty little surprises such as cockroaches and lizards. We didn't need to ask who was paying for the hotels – it was already decided that my dad was footing the bill. Without the English pound, my relatives could never have been able to afford the opportunity of going sightseeing in their own country so the luxuries had to be kept to a minimum.

I have many happy memories of our days around the north west of India. Despite the poverty, the colours and smiles of the people and the rich historic culture of the country made it an interesting and enriching experience. I could devote the whole book to the vast traditions, cultures and history that we experienced, however, this would not allow me to move on to the next chapter in my life so the jewels of India will have to wait. However, I cannot continue without mentioning the postcard picture view of the Taj Mahal that captivated me as soon as I set eyes on it.

We stepped out of our van excited that we were about to see the wonder of the world that we had seen so many times on the television. First, we were confronted by intimidating brown-bricked arches. There was no sign of the Taj Mahal and we were somewhat disappointed that the great white palace wasn't the first thing we saw. But as we walked under the archway, there it stood in all its majesty. Its gardens and long runway of water in front of it were perfectly symmetrical, working with the towering Taj Mahal to create a unique and graceful sight. I remember being struck with awe at its perfection.

We walked inside where we could see the tombs of Moneeba Mahal and Shah Jahan. Shah Jahan, an infamous and charismatic Moghul, had built the Taj in memory of his most loved wife. The sparkling white marble felt hot under our bare feet – having taken our shoes off before entrance in to the tomb courtyard out of respect. Once we had visited the tomb we spent some time exploring the gardens and cooling ourselves down near the fountains. Despite the colour of our skin, it was clear to the tourist hunting photographers that we were their next prey. And like typical tourists, we were drawn in by their persuasive, cheap prices. Soon, we were part of the tourist crowd, creating poses that made us look like we were holding the Taj by its crescent on the head of its dome!

A few hundred metres away from the Taj Mahal was the fort to which Shah Jahan's son had exiled him, soon after he had built the beautiful mausoleum for his late wife. As we stared out of the same window that the Moghul had looked through, we could still appreciate the beauty of the Taj Mahal despite its distance, just as the grieving Moghul had done.

Rasool Allah SAW Said: *When a husband and wife look at each other with Love, Allah looks at both with Mercy.*
(Bukhari 6:19 and Tirmidhi 14:79)

Agra was our last stop and once we left the Taj Mahal we were on our journey back home to the village of Dayadra. The palaces of Rajasthan were full of architectural beauty and despite my younger sister suffering a serious case of diarrhoea, we managed to appreciate them. The capital city of Rajasthan – Jaipur, with its tall, pink walls and many forts and temples challenged our concept of a city. It was also overrun by monkeys, especially around the temples and other areas of interest: areas where there were ample tourists to provide ample nourishment. They also have a holy status in India due to their close likeness to the monkey god Hanuman, so, like the cows, they were allowed to roam free, providing entertainment for the tourists and causing disruption for the locals.

Once home I settled back into the monotony of village life. Despite the many days that I had lived in the village, my immaturity and slight superiority complex restricted my sense of adventure. There was no external snobbery as I could easily mix in with my Indian family and the many families that we had visited, however, internally there was a misguided notion of patriarchal superiority that didn't allow me to completely relax and enjoy the privilege of such a unique holiday.

I listened to George Michael in our bedroom, wrote in my diary and stared out of the window, observing the locals. One day I was invited to visit the local high school. My curiosity motivated me to accept and I found myself sitting at a desk in a sparse room with over fifty students and one teacher. The students were silent. There was no fidgeting or whispering. Corporal punishment was, and still is, legal and I presumed that it was the threat of a beating that maintained the silence and respect that was no longer guaranteed back home. In my ignorance, when

151

asked to stand up and talk about myself, I started speaking in fluent English. The teacher quickly stopped me and asked me to speak in Guajarati as the students were not yet fluent English speakers. It was the first time that I had to speak in front of a formal audience in my mother tongue and I found myself stumbling on my own words. After some small talk with the students I was escorted back home.

The differences between England and India in all areas of living and learning were surfacing daily. This vast contradiction in the standards of living compared to back home were a potent reminder for all of us to appreciate our place of birth and the many advantages that have come with it. Ignorance is bliss - as the locals demonstrated. Their meagre means of surviving did not make them unhappy as they had never experienced 'a better life' than the one they were living and so they had nothing to compare their lives with. However, I found myself constantly referring each and every experience back to my own life and it was this that was ultimately preventing me from appreciating every moment to its true potential.

We were now counting down the days to our return back home. Time was moving at a slow place. We were four weeks into the holiday and the two weeks that stood between us and our much missed home seemed like an eternity. We were fantasising about eating fish and chips with curry sauce and re-living those cosy moments when we step out from the cold into the warmth of a heated room. Our familiar world seemed out of reach and our impatience was beginning to show. But just as soon as we began to protest about our boredom my dad announced that we were to embark on another adventure, this time to the south of Gujarat – to revisit the city of Bombay that as yet we had only caught a glimpse of.

Once again we were joined by a sprinkling of cousins and an uncle or two but this time we were not subjected to the cramp conditions of the Maruti. Instead, we found ourselves using the infamous Indian railway system for the second time. My dad's budget was clearly getting tight as we were demoted from first class down to second class – a definite stumble in the line of hierarchical travel, however it wasn't a total disaster, as second class was followed by third class and after this, there was always the roof of the train!

The bright blue leather seats were relatively comfortable and the sleepers above the seats were occupied with tired travellers attempting to catch some sleep under the loud, whirring fans that substituted for air conditioning. Ants and flies shared our space and a wide variety of travellers ranging from the businessman to the slum inhabitant were making their way to Bombay. We had now become accustomed to the creepy crawlies and the novelty of seeing the two extremes of human society sharing the same environment, and so we sat back and allowed the food vendors and beggars to pass us by as we took in the scenery and day-dreamed about all the home comforts that we would soon be enjoying.

Within a few hours we were outside Victoria Station and climbing in to the classic black and yellow Bombay taxi. We travelled down the same roads and witnessed the same scenes of poverty that we had seen the first time round, except this time, the shock factor had worn off. When we were near our hotel, we walked past the slum homes on the side of the paths and peered into their lives. Some of these homes had ingeniously installed portable televisions in to their tiny spaces and they were sat around as a family intently watching Bollywood movies. Others were taking a nap or having a wash. They were immune to the voyeuristic element of their lives as they made the best of what had been handed to them – yet in my self-absorbed head, I was praying for a decent hotel, with a high hygiene standard and a toilet that had a toilet seat rather than having to make do with a glorified hole in the ground!

It was getting more and more evident that my dad's budget was coming to an end. Our hotel was to be the 'musafir khana' – the place where most British Muslims from the Gujarat area stayed when visiting Bombay. The building itself blended in far too easily with the surrounding buildings, which was slightly worrying. Once inside, there was a stench of urine mixed with bleach and a stifling humidity that was combined with the aroma of male sweat glands. My dad sensed our disappointment and reassured us that our room was to be first class and would not reflect the environment we were enduring at present.

We walked up the mouldy stairs preparing ourselves for disappointment. However, the room was not as horrific as our imagination had led us to believe. The air conditioning and the en-suite bathroom with its smell of freshly sprayed freshener put our fears to bay. We were to spend three nights in this room, and despite the oversized cockroaches that scurried along the floor in the middle of the night, we managed to relax and enjoy what was our final stint as tourists.

Our first day as Bombay tourists was mainly occupied with clothes shopping and, compared to the prices back home; it seemed that they were virtually giving them away for free! The joy on our faces as we were rooting around the glorious bargains must have been obvious, as my dad quickly warned us not to advertise our tourist status so blatantly. The shopkeepers were very apt at spotting a foreign bargain hunter and the price tags on their merchandise would double instantly. And so, we calmed ourselves down and observed as my dad played the bartering game with every item of clothing that we intended to buy. Most of the original prices were cut by over half and yet there was still a little room for negotiation. Shopping in India clearly required a strong will and the skill to negotiate way beyond what would seem reasonable in England. By the end of the day we had worked through the main shopping areas of Bombay and had a collection of clothes substantial enough to last us for over a year!

Whilst working our way through the streets of Bombay we continued to witness the two extremes of Indian society. Limbless beggars approached us around every corner whilst high fashion women walked past us with arms weighed down by multiple shopping bags. In such a short space of time even we were becoming accustomed to the contrasting nature of Indian society so it is no wonder that Indians themselves seemed to be so comfortable with the harshness and cruelty of their social system.

The next day we spent all our time in the more affluent areas of Bombay. We posed in front of the Gate of India and took a boat trip out on the Arabian Sea. On our return we went for a meal at the five stars Taj Hotel that is situated opposite the Gate of India. In such a grand setting, our British tourist status was not enough to help us blend in to the background. Many of the guests were the light skinned variety and even in our parent's home country, we were looked down upon as mere commoners. The fact that my Indian uncle couldn't use a knife and fork only helped to support that misguided image!

It was an uncomfortable meal. We felt like our every move was being observed and so, we ended the meal quickly, paid the extortionate bill and left the hotel. The shops outside were a stark contrast to the day before when we were shopping in the middle of downtown Bombay. This was more like the posh side of British. Amongst the shops was a delicatessen filled to the brim with delicious, irresistible cakes. After grabbing some rupees from my dad, I rushed in and headed straight for the chocolate slice. It was going to cost me three pounds. That was the same as the price of a meal for five in downtown Bombay! Despite the ridiculous price, I justified its purchase by telling myself that I would pay the same back home. Within minutes I had devoured every single crumb and only then did I leave the shop, keeping quiet about my indulgence in some of the Britishness that we were all missing so much.

After our overly sophisticated lunch, we were driven to an open air Bollywood film studio. My interest in all things Bollywood had waned since my discovery of Hollywood – the highly choreographed dancing around trees and the predictable story lines no longer filled my heart with joy or tugged at my naïve heartstrings. Nevertheless, the shouts of 'action' and the random scenes of fighting around a tired looking horse cart did make the visit interesting. Amongst the actors were Salman Khan, Amir Khan, Jeetendra, Pran and Rishi Kapoor – all big names in the Bollywood industry at the time and some of them are still going strong. My dad suggested that we take a picture with the most popular actor at that time, Salman Khan. He wore bright blue trousers – a fashion disaster in my eyes, yet to the Indian film going population Salman Khan has always been seen as a trendsetter. I was elected to do the honour and so, as he completed his dance sequence with the heroine of the film 'Love,' I asked him in an extremely polite manner if I could take a picture with him. His response was one of silence. He simply flicked his fly-away fringe and turned his face towards our camera. I shuffled next to him and the camera went click. As soon as we were done he moved away without any form of acknowledgement that I existed. Being British, I said thank you anyway and we continued on with our tour.

There were only a handful of tourists looking in to the actors at work. Later, I realised that maybe my dad hadn't quite come to the end of his budget, as the fee for visiting the studios must have been substantial considering the status of the actors. Although didn't appreciate the magnitude of the visit at the time, when we returned home we received a big reaction from the Bollywood fans, especially about the fact that we had set eyes on the new big thing in the industry, Salman Khan. My mum's friends, who were unfamiliar with this new blue-trousered, hair-flicking hero, presumed after seeing the photograph that my parents had fixed up my marriage with him! How my life would have been different if that really had been the case!

Our final stint of tourism took us to the beaches of Bombay. A horse and carriage rode us down the famous Marine Drive with the Arabian Sea on one side and affluent hotels and apartments on the other. We stopped at the Chowpadi beach and yet again we let disappoint seep in to us. This was not the brochure image of a beach that was conditioned into our psyche: the sand was flat and a dull brown colour, not golden at all; the sea looked murky and was heavily populated with fully dressed Indians splashing about and talking far too loudly, not at all like the images in the brochures of clear green waters with not another human in sight.

However, being accustomed to disappoint, we remained in good spirits and indulged in the tourist trap activities that awaited us. First, we were to try the famous Bel Puri that was sold in amongst the many food stalls at the edge of the beach. This snack consists of puffed rice filled with savoury vegetables and a tangy tamarind. It was delicious and is still a popular attraction on the beach today.

There were many fresh fruit stalls and we had yet another opportunity to enjoy the sweet, ripe mangoes. Once our stomachs were full and as dusk was approaching my dad called a couple of men over with their horses. We were to experience riding a horse along the beach front as the sun was setting in the background; a romantic notion that was far from the reality that was awaiting us. Only my older sister and I volunteered to take the challenge of sitting on a horse for the first time in our lives – in fact it was the first time that we had ever even touched a horse or stood close to one. The men helped us to mount and soon we were trotting happily along the beach, dodging people and debris along the way. My man with the horse must have considered my relaxed exterior as a sign of confidence as he now upped the gear of the horse from second to third! The gentle trot gathered momentum and I found my bottom bouncing rhythmically on the saddle of the horse as it galloped along the beach. I panicked and shouted at the man to slow it down but my cries of panic fell on deaf ears. Eventually, my adventure of the equestrian variety came to an end and I vowed never to trust a man with a horse on a foreign beach ever again!

On our final day in Bombay we found ourselves at another beach – Juhu beach. This time, our preconceptions were matched with the reality in front of us. Blue-green waters lapped at the golden sands and there was hardly a person in sight. This was clearly the beach reserved for the more sophisticated, financially unchallenged Indian. We relaxed on deck chairs, keeping our traditional Indian attire intact. For lunch, we gathered around a supersize hotplate where we watched our food being cooked – a spicy vegetable curry with fresh naans, served with a delicious choice of cold, refreshing mocktails. This was living it up – delicious food with a fabulous view and a relaxed, family atmosphere away from the realities of the life back home.

Our time in Bombay had ended and we boarded the train that was to take us back to the village of Dayadra. We only had a few days left and they were soon taken up by farewell dinners. Visitors came with letters and small packages that they asked my parents to bring back to England for their family that had also followed the path that my parents had taken.

Our six weeks in India had ended. Despite our desperation to leave the country we did feel that we were given the opportunity to go back to our roots and, even though India was a stark contrast to our lives in England, we now knew what our parents had left behind and could appreciate the difficulty they must have experienced in adjusting to a life so far from their childhood homes.

Landing in Manchester was one of the happiest moments of my life! The cool air and miserable view of the damp weather was a welcomed sight. We relished the need to wear a jacket and sat back without fear in the smooth running car that travelled along a quiet, well-organised motorway where the drivers valued theirs and other road user's lives! Finally, we were back to civilisation.

Chapter Twenty-one

The road to change.

For the first time in my life I had a summer to talk about. I had had an interesting six weeks despite the culture shock and for once, I could talk about more than just a day trip to Blackpool. There were plenty of photos displaying our diverse experiences and in the early nineties it was still relatively uncommon for a family to spend a whole summer abroad. The attention and envy was a pleasurable experience that pushed my self-confidence to a new level.

As my time in sixth form ended, my insecurities were also making their way out of my psyche. I was beginning to recognise myself as an individual who had the option to maintain my own personality whatever circumstance I found myself in. I was beginning to believe in myself: an inner confidence told me that I had the power to make my life one of happiness and independence - a life that was to contrast the one of my parents who seemed to be surviving life rather than living it. Getting the grades required to get in to university was the first step towards this common goal of achieving a life of contentment and security that most of us strive for.

At home, we were still far from scoring the common goal

of contentment. There were periods of relative calm, but the threat of violence always hung in the air. Bouts of gambling still dominated my dad's life and so, we continued to support our mum by fulfilling our role as the 'domestic violence police' as well as supporting her financially by making Christmas crackers at home.

It was also becoming evident that my siblings and I were no longer the young, timid creatures that used to feel intimidated by our dad. Physically, we were stronger and our confidence in the outside world was now making its way in to our home life. One evening, my mum was sitting on the floor as usual, pulling at the string attached to the skirting board for the purpose of cracker making. My uncle was discussing a family matter with my dad when my mum took it upon herself to interject with her opinion on the matter. Her viewpoint was quickly dismissed but unfortunately she persisted in expressing her opinion. At this point I walked into the room and instantly sensed the looming threat of violence. Within seconds, my dad lunged himself off the sofa and was about to grab a folded chair that was intended to cause my mum yet more pain. I instinctively wrapped my arms around my dad's waist and physically pulled him back down on the sofa. He screamed my name and told me to release him, but my grip remained firm till I felt the threat of violence ease.

It was the first time that I had attempted to control my dad physically. The usual plan of action involved removing my mum from the situation but confidence and physical strength resulted in a more effective reaction. My dad was shocked by my behaviour and for a while, he was stunned in to silence. I felt exhilarated as well as surprised by the fire within me that managed to overpower the ugly, violent side of my dad and for the first time I felt a sense of empowerment concerning the domestic abuse that had dominated our home life.

My brothers were also now fully-fledged teenagers and the only male role model in their lives had let them down. The textbook dad prescribed a strong, authoritative man who had the ability to communicate with his children, showing sensitivity when required and providing a safe, nurturing family environment for them to grow up in. Instead, my brothers witnessed a dad that was addicted to gambling – a dad that mistreated his wife and a dad that was restricted from ambition. Their young minds had absorbed this pattern of behaviour throughout their lives and as they got older, their own behaviour reflected what they had witnessed.

Gambling was an addiction that both my brothers succumbed to. They spent their spare time at the bookmakers or huddled around fruit machines. Although their addictions were not as severe as my dad's they still managed to accrue debts with their friends that they couldn't pay back. When desperate, my older brother even resorted to stealing from our home. Over a thousand pounds was taken from a chest of drawers in one of the bedrooms, and when the theft was discovered my dad's anger was unleashed with a fury that we rarely witnessed when it came to his children.

A snooker cue was the weapon that my dad waved around as he chased my brother around the house. He was angry, but more than that he was utterly distraught: distraught that his sons were following in his own footsteps. After several rounds of running and screaming, my dad eventually managed to take a hold of my brother. He raised the snooker cue and for the first time in his life, used violence against his eldest son. The cue gave out a loud thud as it landed on my brother's back. Next, amidst the screams of pain and our desperate pleas for the chaos to stop, my dad gave my brother his marching orders. He was to leave the house and never come back. Stealing from the family home was a crime beyond forgiveness and the solution was to dismiss the culprit without any form of communication or explanation.

My brother left the house. We were dumbstruck. The anger in my dad's eyes was terrifying and his frustrations hadn't yet been released. Our violence radar detected more abuse so my mum and the four of us remaining siblings ran around the kitchen on to the staircase. We all sat on the stairs in a state of fear, praying that an end to the violence was coming. I remember my legs shaking in fear as my dad tried to open the door that stood between us and his anger.

Fortunately the door had a lock on it and my mum quickly shut the bolt. We heard my dad's heavy footsteps heading towards us and after failing to open the door in the conventional way he lunged at the door with his foot, cracking the wood and making a heavy dent. We let out a cry of panic as we imagined the horrific scene that would follow if he managed to get through, but at that point my dad went quiet. We remained still, deeply suspicious of the calm after what had been a display of utter terror and threatening behaviour.

After waiting silently on the stairs for a few minutes we heard a quiet sobbing: it was coming from my dad. Sitting on the sofa with his knees tight around his chest, my dad was slowly rocking back and forth crying. The realisation that his son had become so desperate that he had to steal from his own family hit him hard. This was the first time that he saw a direct consequence of his behaviour on one of his children. It was also the first time that I had witnessed my dad's vulnerability. Despite his earlier behaviour, I felt sorry for him. Seeing a grown man cry is very much an emotional experience but when it is your own dad you feel a natural desire to console and comfort – yet we didn't know how. It was a rare occurrence to demonstrate love in our family and despite my instincts telling me to go ahead and put my arms around him, the reality of the situation was a world away. We left him on his own, confused about how to feel, and tried to continue with our day.

My brother stayed away from the house for several days having safely found refuge at the house of our uncle who lived opposite. Like every other dramatic incident that happened to us, this incident was also forgotten quickly and we continued with our lives, accepting that this is how it has always been and how it always will be. Life continued without any discussion between my dad and brother. The relationships involving my dad and us siblings never seemed to evolve as there was always the fear that he wouldn't be able to cope with the truth and indirectly, we would be the cause of yet another story of abuse.

Another incident that highlighted the unfortunate reality of a son picking up his dad's habits happened during Ramadan when my dad was abroad. We were about to break the fast when my brother insisted upon an onion salad to go with his curry. It had only been a few minutes since sun set and we were all absorbed in the task of filling our bellies and were therefore reluctant to fulfil his request. My brother persisted in his command and eventually my mum asked my older sister to prepare the salad. After a short whinging session she brought the salad to him. By now he was half way through his curry and he considered the salad to have arrived too late. He violently grabbed the plate from my sister then threw all the contents angrily at her face after which he slammed the plate on the floor. We were shocked but not scared. This demonstration of anger was not unusual in our home but with my dad being abroad, we were expecting to have a quiet Ramadan. Instantly, we all started screaming and sobbing at my brother: what was he doing? What was the point of dad being away when we had him to take over? We threw a barrage of insults and frustrations at him, making it clear that we were not looking for a replacement of our dad.

My brother got up and left the house. He stood outside, easing the stress with a cigarette, when one of his friends approached him. He also lit up and he then asked my brother to explain about the guilt that was written all over his face. As my brother re-lived the incident his friend lowered the butt of his still burning cigarette and singed my brother's hand with it. It was the reaction of a good friend to help stop my brother's idiotic behaviour. He was told that this was what was going to happen to him if he ever attempted to hurt those that he supposedly loved ever again. My brother recalls this moment as life changing as it made him realise the disastrous consequences of becoming a clone of our dad. It was cowardly and the shame that he felt ensured that he never displayed such uncalled for, irrational behaviour again.

My older brother was now eighteen and physically he was taller and stronger than my dad. As we got older our bond strengthened, having shared and developed the same emotions and tactics needed to defend our mum. We were approaching the inevitable climax of a house accustomed to abuse – a united front against the abuser. The classic scenario is an easy one to picture: my dad on one side of the room with his fists up, ready to take his frustrations out on my mum; on the other side of the room a scared, tired mother surrounded by five protective children determined that this time it would be their dad who would lose the fight. My older brother stepped forward and filled his chest up with air hoping to look intimidating. With his most grown up voice he told my dad that he would have to go through him before he could get to our mum. We all looked at him, proud of ourselves that finally we were able to protect our mum. We were confident that we could overpower our dad.

My dad hesitated. His fists gradually made their way back down. The anger drained from his face as he realised that he was no longer the dominant male in the house. His reaction only gave us more confidence to stand our ground. Soon, my dad had backed off and was again left sitting on the sofa playing back the many reasons that had led to the confrontation that was to change things forever.

After this scene was played out, the threat of abuse was dramatically reduced. We were maturing into young adults and the fear that used to live permanently in our hearts was subsiding. We could devote more of our energies into our own lives and begin the job of setting up a future for ourselves that would exclude any form of threatening behaviour.

Chapter Twenty-two

University days

I managed to accrue the exact number of points required to enter in to what was then Manchester Polytechnic. My course was a BA major in English and minor in social history. There was no question of us moving away to study. My older sister was in her final year of studying at the university down the road and now I had joined her in the daily twenty minute commute by train between Manchester and Bolton. It was already a rare occurrence for families to send their daughters to university without the added fear of their daughters moving away from home.

We were the first in our community to attend university thanks to my dad's advanced attitude that even as women, we needed to be independent. He always told us that an education at degree level would allow our process of absorbing and interpreting information reach a more sophisticated level and that our perspective on life would develop intellectually. There was no pressure to become lawyers or doctors at the end of our education – my dad claimed that he would be happy if we ended up sweeping the streets as long as our outlook on life and our attitude towards others superseded beyond the simple.

This intellectual viewpoint reflected a large part of my

dad's personality. He had never had the opportunity to use his intelligence in the wider world to achieve personal goals and ambitions but in spite of this his best conversations were always the ones that involved a higher level of understanding. Because of this love of knowledge my dad made our journey in to higher education a smooth one. My mum's ambition for us was a traditional one – to work a simple job after school so that we could be occupied with the business of saving money for our wedding! It was only when we became professionals that she realised the importance of an education, even for mere girls.

Unfortunately, my brothers did not appreciate the opportunities opening up in front of them. They spent many of their college days out of college, choosing to visit the bookies instead. Before they completed their 'studies' at college they were given an ultimatum by my dad to either take their courses seriously or to find a job. Without their willingness to commit to either, my dad made the choice for them and they were forced to enter the world of work.

Sameena was also lucky enough to achieve the grades and have the supportive family needed to get ahead. Unfortunately, she was at the 'proper' university down the road as opposed to the polytechnic, so although we would sometimes meet on our commute, we no longer enjoyed the daily security that our friendship provided.

My life at university didn't quite live up to the image of

the slobby, alcohol infused student who consumed cold pizza for breakfast and shared a fridge full of labelled food. Living at home meant that my life remained the same. I made new friends and became very familiar with the railway system but at the end of the day I found myself sleeping in my own bed and still enjoying my mum's cooking.

My choice of course was not the usual subject that Asian families opted for at that time. English was not specifically designed for a future career, unlike business studies, law or medicine and even though my course was the most popular one at the polytechnic, I was the only Asian person to have chosen to study it. Initially, the stark absence of brown skin came as a shock. My circle of friends always consisted of people that shared my religion and culture: there was never any need for explanations and I had become accustomed to non-judgemental company.

I now found myself with a circle of non-Muslim, white friends. The transition from the familiar to the new was not as difficult as I had anticipated. Within a few weeks I had a new circle of friends exclusively reserved for university. Our discussions were interesting and varied but still a world away from the ones that I had been used to. I mentioned my religious background to my new circle of friends and although there was no judgement, through no fault of their own, the mutual experience and understanding was missing. When religion dictates how you live your life, it is difficult to make a deep connection with a non-believer. However, my relationships were still fulfilling and progressive – it was my religious beliefs that became stagnant, fumbling in the background as the mention of God became less and less frequent in my daily life.

One of my closer friends at university was Samantha. We were together for many of our lectures and tutorials. It was through her that I caught a glimpse of how the student away from home lived. It wasn't until the beginning of the third year of my studies that I plucked up enough courage to begin planning nights out with Samantha. For these nights out I had to find a way to stay overnight in Manchester, which involved a certain degree of deception on my part.

At home, I managed to convince my mum that Samantha was obliged to spend the night on her own as her housemates were all going back to their home towns. I explained the fear that my friend felt at the thought of being all alone in an empty, quiet house. It was the responsible thing for me to do to offer to help her out, accompanying her in her time of need. My mum didn't take much convincing and she allowed me to go ahead as long as my dad approved.

My dad used the same line that he often used when we

requested permission to release ourselves in to the wider world: I trust you, but I don't trust the world. Again, I heard the familiar line. I listened to his reasons as to why spending the night away from home could lead to many temptations and how he was putting his trust in me not to take advantage of him allowing us to make the choices that would confront us. After the usual spiel he released his leash and I was allowed to accompany my lonely friend. I knew that I had withheld the real reason for my night away from home and I had an inkling that my dad could sense my transparency, but I truly respected the freedom that I was being given. It was rare for a Muslim girl to spend a night away from home, in another town, with a non-relation, but yet I was given this privilege.

These occasional nights of freedom were an opportunity for me to experience the night-life that my fellow students often boasted about. Our routine would be to go to Samantha's house after lectures, have some tea, turn the music up loud and enjoy a pre-session before we experienced the real thing. My objective for the night would be to thoroughly immerse myself in to the music and soak in the atmosphere. My long plait of hair remained intact and my style of dress, which had now moved on from the traditional to the western, consisted of a pair of jeans and a T-shirt.

We spent most of our nights of freedom at the glorified

student nightclub. During my first time at the night-club, I experienced moments of panic where I would stop dancing and look around in fear that my dad would turn up and drag me by my plait in a fiery rage out of the night club!

The balance of Asian girls and boys was heavily disproportionate. A large group of the Asian boys – mainly Muslims, would loiter in the corner, staring at the talent on offer. They scoured the club hoping for eye contact – an open invitation to a drunken kiss. None of them had the intention to dance – their motive was to pull indiscriminately – to achieve some sort of success with the opposite sex. Initially, I found their blatant motives shocking but then I realised that many of the club go-ers hoped for some sort of success - even if their motives weren't as obvious. I reflected on the impression that I must have given simply for being there. My motives were very clear to me – I was simply there to dance. I had no interest in alcohol or boys, but just the fact that I was there suggested otherwise. Several times, boys would hang around me whilst I was dancing. They would try to make eye contact, but my refusal to even acknowledge their existence would ensure that they moved on to their next prospect.

The nightclub environment was fumigated with alcohol and sweat – a world away from the romantic notions of the perfect first kiss that I had repeatedly envisioned in my head. The sleazy nature of the alcohol infused kissing couples was not a pretty sight and I avoided all close proximity with them. There were many negatives about a typical student clubbing night; however, my desire to dance and lose myself for a few hours outweighed the sticky floors and alcoholic fumes.

So where was God during my moments of rebellion?

The Prophet said, "*To know what is right and to fail to act is as grave as a false action.*"

Although His presence wasn't at the forefront of my mind, He was always a part of my subconscious. There were many factors that made my nightclub experiences purely opportunities to dance. Despite the lies, I was still very much aware of the trust put upon me by my dad and I didn't want to betray him further. There was no natural desire within me to experiment with alcohol or boys and I felt a genuine disgust with both when in the nightclub environment. My religious upbringing, that always put good morals and modest behaviour at the forefront of my life, heavily influenced this attitude. This moralistic uptake wasn't exclusive to my Muslim status – Samantha was also keen to stay away from alcohol instigated snogs and although she did drink, I had never witnessed her drink herself beyond tipsy. I had very few feelings of envy and was satisfied with taking the occasional dip in to the nightlife of the student.

The Prophet said, *"When a man is at peace with his conscience, he has no real enemy."*

Away from the nightclubs, student life did offer a world of independence that I knew I would never experience as a single woman. I had relative freedom at home and I was happy with how my life was unfolding, but the concept of being myself without any pressures or influences from my family or community seemed attractive. It was another fantasy that remained firmly in my imagination and looking back, I have no regrets about the fantasy that never became a reality.

The three years of my degree passed by without drama. I was intellectually stimulated with the textual analysis of medieval literature and analytical discussions about the theories of Sigmund Freud. I also had many opportunities to develop my creative writing skills, and although I was never top of the class, occasionally I produced masterpieces that achieved 1st class grades. A write-up of my own version of a scene from one of Shakespeare's plays was a memorable highlight, but even more impressive was my twenty thousand word dissertation on the historical changes of the Bollywood industry over half a decade. It was this masterpiece that pushed my borderline pass rate from a 2:2 to a 2:1 and earned its pride of place in the university library as an example of an exceptionally good piece of work.

I was to be promoted to the 'proper' university up the road the following academic year, even though by now the polytechnic was re-named the Manchester Metropolitan University. I had decided on a career in teaching – not so much a calling but a possibility that I had always considered and without a desire to follow any other career path I decided to take the plunge and immerse myself in to a Postgraduate in primary teaching – a course that required the attendance of lectures eight hours a day as opposed to the eight hours a week that I was accustomed to.

I began my course at the age of 21. Three years of experience as a university student had done wonders for my confidence and my intellect. My self esteem and maturity was continuing to grow as I experienced new people and found myself challenged by new situations. The P.G.C.E took me to three different schools where I had to prove my ability to discipline as well as stimulate a class of thirty young children. The intensity of the course was sometimes overwhelming, however, throughout its duration I had no doubts about having made the right choice of career.

It was during my P.G.C.E that I re-united with a former sixth form student, Sahila, who is now one of my dearest friends. Despite our status of virtual strangers at the college we quickly found common ground that we could build upon.

My P.G.C.E year was the most challenging year of my life in terms of the moralistic dilemmas that presented themselves to me. Although from a western point of view, my moments of rebellion were considered the norm, from my personal perspective, they were a betrayal to my family, my community and to my deeply rooted beliefs. Generations have passed since my young years of inexperience and the choices that I was faced with seem incomparable to the ones facing young Muslims today, however, every moment, past, present and future is unique to its owner and the mixed emotions of joy, guilt and the sense of a betrayal to myself were very much real at the time.

During my P.G.C.E year I spent many a happy afternoon in the student pub, enjoying the company of friends and showing off my new-found confidence with witty banter and flirtatious mannerisms. This outward display of what seemed like alcohol infused behaviour attracted the attention from the male students and discovering that I had not touched a drop of alcohol only served to make that attraction stronger.

Despite my new-found flirtations, I still kept my eyes firmly fixed away from the stare of the opposite sex. However, the inevitable time came when someone approached me and the lure of his spine tingling compliments became too difficult for me to resist.

His name was Peter: tall, slim, a well-to-do history student who found me fascinating. He approached me in the pub, beginning the conversation by asking me if I was drunk. When I replied to the negative he expressed his disbelief that I could be so loud and expressive without any influence of alcohol. After that, he remained seated with my group of friends and spent most of his time staring at me. I genuinely believed that despite my confidence about how my life was turning out, there was nothing particular attractive about me. Yet here he was, a good looking, intelligent and sane boy who wanted to get to know me better. His piercing stare was difficult to ignore and I knew that at the age of 22, I had a possible candidate for my first kiss.

I agreed to meet him for lunch. It was an easy decision. The parents, my religion and God didn't get a look in. My self-esteem was sky-high and the tingling that ran all through my body when I re-lived the moment that I met Peter repeatedly confirmed that I should go ahead and act upon my instincts. I always knew that if I analysed the situation too deeply I would walk away from it, ending an adventure that had hardly begun.

We talked for hours. His life-style away from the university was a world away from mine yet he found my background intriguing. He did most of the listening as I told him about my family and my experiences growing up in a community foreign to him. We were sharing something special and, without the risk of sounding like a Mills and Boons novel, there was a definite excitement as our body language became more expressive of the chemistry building up between us.

Eventually, he asked me back to his halls for a drink. I quickly accepted and I found myself sat on the floor in his room listening to The Stone Roses. The hypnotic tracks helped to calm my nerves. Adrenalin rushed through my body as I waited in anticipation to experience another momentous rite of passage.

It was a monumental disappointment! 'Electricity flows, like the very first kiss' – that's what the rock chick claims in the famous pop song, but the only thing flowing between us was saliva! The previous thick atmosphere of lust and romance was now followed by an incredible anticlimax. Either the concept of the first kiss was over-hyped or the two of us had got the technique completely wrong. I had nothing to compare the failed kiss with, so I decided to blame Peter for my lack of enjoyment. Within a few moments, the build-up of excitement and hormones had come to a miserable end. I was determined to avoid a second try in case of yet another failure, so we took the safe option of holding hands. Eventually, I left the halls and as we hugged each other, we knew that we were never going to see each other again.

An opportunity to redeem the disappointment did come my way one more time before I left the student world behind. Simon had asked my friend several times to introduce him to me and eventually he got his way. We engaged in stimulating conversations the few times that we met up and, as the chemistry developed, it was myself that instigated the kiss – much to my friend Samantha's surprise, who had never seen me behave with such malice before. We were in the pub and I could feel the chemistry between us. As our circle of friends continued to talk, I grabbed his hand and led him to the cloakroom. We spent the rest of the evening in our own bubble of lust and flirtation and as the evening came to an end, we both knew that there was no point of attempting to develop a relationship, and so, we took our time in saying goodbye to our short but exciting love affair.

I always knew that nurturing and growing a relationship with a non-Muslim would be a futile passion. My conscience would question me every step of the way, causing guilt, fear, a constant stream of betrayal and most importantly the living of a life that was a lie to my very own beliefs and way of existence. This definite look in to the future is what made the decisions to end relationships before they even began such an easy task.

I had to own up to myself that my actions went against everything that I believed in. Two innocent encounters may seem harmless to the Western eye, but for me, it was a disloyalty to my spirituality. I had taken a small step into the world forbidden by Islam – a world where, despite the seemingly harmless nature of my acts, I could have allowed my passions to snowball in to a frenzy of non-Islamic acts. I am, and will always be eternally grateful to God for giving me the heart and strength to submit only to Him as the opportunities to answer my carnal desires and to follow what Western society suggested was the norm, continued to open up in front of me.

Sameena was still a big part of my life, and confessing my behaviour to her was one of the hardest things that I have ever done. We were at a wedding and as usual, boredom had set in, so we decided to escape the mass of gossiping ladies by going for a cruise in Sameena's car. Nerves set in as I realised that this was my opportunity to tell all. Once confession was over, Sameena parked up and said very little. Just like Samantha, she was also shocked with my out-of-character behaviour. Her disbelief confirmed my own realisation that I was not betraying just those around me, but also myself. Islam requires consistency to be effective – a consistency of actions that reflect the words of God. By playing with my life, I was playing with the message that Islam seeks to send and I knew then that by ignoring what I recognised to be the divine truth would only serve to injure my own self.

When something weighs on your conscience, give it up.
(Prophet Muhammad (s) in Al-Tirmidhi, Hadith 8.)

A true action leads to the path of virtue and good deeds, and virtue paves the way of a person to Paradise, and the said person continues to speak the truth till in the sight of Allah he is named Siddiq or Truthful. Lying leads to vice, and vice leads to indecent acts and if a person goes on lying till in the sight of Allah he is named a liar.

(The Prophet (s) as reported by Abdullah Ibn Mas'ud (r) in Bukhari and Muslim.)

Chapter Twenty-three

The world of work

My university days had ended and two days before the end of the academic year, after countless unsuccessful applications and several failed interviews I managed to secure myself a two-term maternity contract at a primary school. I had now officially left the world without responsibilities and had walked into the adult world where rules and bureaucracy were a part of daily life. This constrained work environment had its advantages as it bought with it an attractive pay packet. Once my first salary was transferred in to my bank account I told my mum that we no longer needed to spend hours pulling strings to earn the same monthly wage that I was now earning in a week.

Although my first post in teaching demanded dedication and enthusiasm, it was a world away from the intensity of the P.G.C.E. I quickly found my feet and discovered that I had a natural talent at owning and controlling my immediate classroom environment. Despite the young age of the children they responded to my authoritative style of teaching, allowing them to make maximum progression whilst maintaining a calm working atmosphere.

To complete my first year of teaching I applied for and received an interview for a one-term contract at a junior school. With two terms of experience behind me I was able to secure the job by giving detailed answers to the many questions asked. The school's uniform consisted of short trousers, blazers and school logo caps – an image that reflected the intake and expectations of the school. Without any behavioural or academic challenges to deal with, the stress free job seemed unnaturally easy. By the end of the year a permanent post had come up and despite my ability to fill the post, the head teacher advised me to go and get some 'real' experience as her school was one that was more suited to a teacher close to retirement age!

And so I moved on to my final teaching post in Bolton; a three year experience that was to shape my future years as a teacher. The school was situated in the middle of a council estate, and although I was determined to remain professional – avoiding the stereotypical views typically held about council estate residents, it seemed that the residents themselves were very quick to confirm the reality of those prejudices.

I was teaching reception – six and seven year olds. The majority of the class was made up of sweet, immature children, who displayed all the characteristics of innocence and a blissful ignorance of the adult world. However, a handful of them were miniature copies of their unrefined parents whose liberal expressions of their disgust towards any form of authority, discipline or morals were vocalised in no uncertain terms outside the classroom door on a daily basis.

The absence of a good role model in the children's lives was blatantly demonstrated every day: from verbal obscenities in response to an unwanted instruction to random bursts of anger resulting in a trashed classroom and physical removal of the child. This behaviour seemed unnatural in seven year olds, yet their experiences in their short lives had already moulded them, labelling them as 'special needs' children with extreme behavioural difficulties.

However, no blame could be allocated to their young minds. At home time, their parents would have little shame in telling them to 'fucking get a move on' in front of me. The stench of alcohol and cigarettes was common and it was rare to get a parent enquiring about their child's progression. Within the unconventional families were a mother and grandmother who had slept with the same man and produced a child each from him. This unusual sexual activity resulted in two children in my class being related indirectly as uncle and nephew. The list of anti-social behaviour goes on, and although I don't wish to be judgemental, I was clearly witnessing the detrimental affects upon a child's self esteem when they are exposed to an unstable, insecure environment.

On a lighter note, although perhaps just as worrying,

one particular little girl in my class had developed a peculiar taste for all things snotty! Whilst teaching on the carpet, one of my little students let out a tremendous sneeze that resulted in some gooey snot landing on her knee. The girl next to her spotted the pool of green and considering it a tasty snack. She proceeded in attempting to pick it up with her finger and devouring it. Thankfully, I spotted her launch for the grotesque snack and stopped it from entering her mouth just in time!

There were many incidents at the school that developed my professionalism as well as exposing me to the reality and consequences of a community living a life without money or motivation. After the experiences at this school, I was set up for a career that could overcome any behavioural challenge.

My lifestyle was now different. Work had constrained my time and the freedom of a student life had all but diminished. I now looked forward to the weekends and the next wage packet. My social life consisted of shopping, dining out, the cinema and visiting friends. I was happy with my life, enjoying the financial freedom that work allowed and making the most of my free time by indulging in an active social life.

Home life was also settled. Our adult status had put a stop to the violent abuse against my mum. We attempted to move towards becoming a 'normal' family by spending some time in the company of my dad. What could be considered intellectual conversations became a part of our lives – exposing the hidden depths and talents that my dad had kept away from us for such a long time. His well thought out advice always seemed to fall in to place and his views of the world were a reality that we were experiencing every day. These words of wisdom reached far beyond our ears: family members and friends from near and far would look to my dad for advice ranging from what would be the best type of visa to travel to India, to searching for the perfect spouse for their children.

And by the age of twenty-two I had also become a candidate for the arranged marriage. My older brother and sister, who had also gone down the route of allowing my parents to have a major role in choosing their partners, were now married. My older sister wasn't too picky with her choice of husband, as she said she agreed to the seventh proposal and my brother, who always carried a laid back attitude to life, agreed to marry our cousin back in India whom he had met on our trip there.

Before the serious business of finding a husband was to begin, I had the crazy notion in my head that maybe I would be permitted to take a holiday abroad – a real holiday as opposed to a stint in the local village in India: a holiday with a friend rather than my parents. The concept of being abroad without the careful watch of my family and community seemed far out of reach, but I decided to take a risk and suggested the possibility to my dad. His response took me by surprise as he casually answered in the positive, as long as I had the means to finance it. I was quick to act after his response as I knew that time would corrupt his decision when interference from other people would sway his decision towards the negative.

My younger sister also expressed her desire to join me in my first independent adventure away from the watchful eyes of the community. I had enough savings to help her fund the holiday and so, together with our friend Najma, who was an experienced traveller, we decided on our destination and wasted no time getting on that plane!

Chapter Twenty-four

Egyptian fun

At the age of 23 I was taking my second trip abroad: a trip that was going to be the polar opposite of my first foreign experience. We boarded the flight and were in Luxor airport in Egypt within hours. As we boarded the small cruise ship that was going to take us down the river Nile, stopping at the many historical sites along the way, I took a deep breath and took the time to appreciate the situation I was in. It was a rare opportunity for a girl in our community to independently explore the sights and sounds of a world beyond the neighbouring towns, yet here I was, hundreds of miles away from home, doing exactly that. I was determined to take full advantage of the situation by thoroughly enjoying myself whilst remaining within the boundaries of trust that ruled my subconscious.

From the onset, I was aware of the Islamic environment. There was a mosque around every corner and the call to prayer could be heard throughout the day. The local women were dressed modestly and most of the men adopted the Prophet Muhammad's (peace be upon him) form of dress. Yet within this outward show of religiosity was a world filled with all the traps of a country that had tourism as a major source of income: the serving of alcohol and opportunities to mingle with forthcoming tourists whilst working in the small hours under the cover of darkness.

We kept ourselves away from this unfamiliar world – our daily routine on the miniature cruise ship didn't allow for late nights. Every day involved being woken up by a man with a gong just before sunrise. After a swift shower and breakfast, our ship would dock and we visited famous temples such as Karnak, Edfu and Philae. We also managed to squeeze in an early morning start to watch the sun rise in the desert and then onwards to Abu Simbel, all of which was led by an entertaining and very knowledgeable guide. We were in awe of the history that dominated our surroundings. Every magnificent structure told of the archaic beliefs and traditions that ruled Ancient Egypt. The dominating nature of the temples reflected the power and might of its rulers and, thanks to our guide's talents in bringing Egyptian history to life, there never came a dull moment where the sights and stories didn't inspire.

The climate in Egypt was like nothing that I had ever experienced before. Forty five degrees of blazing heat and humidity scorched the rough sands of the temples and forced endless trickles of perspiration to run down our bodies. Our determination to make the most of our holiday motivated us to ignore the sweltering conditions and concentrate on the smells, sights and sounds that enthralled us throughout our historical tour down the Nile.

Within a few days my fellow fifty passengers and I had become familiar with each other. We had developed a special rapport with a select group of passengers and by the end of our cruise adventure we were all part of a role-play drama as the pharaoh and his harem. We constantly referred to our harem of six and enjoyed the banter that went with it. On the themed Egyptian night we all dressed up as Egyptians and pinned the numbers from one to six on our backs, indicating our place in the harem. Wife number one was the real life wife of the 'pharaoh' and from there we were ordered by age. The constant references to our make-believe harem further enhanced our escape from reality as well as creating a relaxed, fun atmosphere.

Between the mini tours of temples and tombs, we relaxed on the boat, taking in many beautiful sunsets and soothing scenes of desert meeting water. We observed young children playing and laughing on the edge of the river, enjoying their youth exactly how nature intended. The locals sat in small groups, smoking hookah and sharing laughter. The laid back serenity of life along the river was a world away from the reality of home and family. This was the first time I was experiencing a true holiday: I was, truly, getting away from it all.

Our journey took us down the Nile to Aswan and back again to Luxor. From there, we said goodbye to Ancient

Egypt and boarded an internal flight to Cairo. Our in-flight entertainment consisted of eyeing up the handsome male flight attendants. They had olive skin, short curly hair and light coloured eyes – yet these men were Muslims! It was an unexpected treat, to be waited on hand and foot by such beautiful members of the human race, and we made the best of it by enjoying the attention that they were so willing to give.

Once in Cairo we were transported to our five star hotel – Ramses II. It was an ostentatious building, both inside and out. Its reception consisted of tall, gilded columns and oversized couches that were dwarfed by the high domed ceilings and elaborately designed floors. The décor was traditional Egyptian with a slight modern twist, making it appealing to the eye whilst maintaining its identity. Throughout our short stay we were treated like royalty, being greeted warmly by every member of staff and having every whim and fancy fulfilled. This was my first experience of living in surroundings far beyond my reality and I was determined to savour each and every moment.

The men in Cairo were beautiful. The tight curls in their hair and light eyes set in olive skin provided plenty of eye candy whilst exploring the sights and sounds of the famous city. We were careful however, not to make our fascination with their exotica too obvious as we were aware that we were also attracting some male attention: the fact that we were clearly not Egyptian aroused curiosity and we were sensible enough to know that if we were to respond with any form of flirtation we would have to deal with the consequences. The unwritten rule of trust and loyalty with regards to our parents quickly put an end to any notions of holiday romances that could easily get out of hand.

We only had two days in Cairo and the two obvious places of interest that we needed to visit were the pyramids and the Egyptian Museum. Without our guide and the company of our harem, we had to make our own way there. Thankfully, our experienced fellow traveller Najma led the way and soon we were being taken by taxi to one of the wonders of the world: The Great Pyramids of Giza. From what we had seen in the brochures, we were expecting to be driven deep in to the desert, however, within twenty minutes we could see them standing tall and proud against modern Cairo.

As soon as we exited the taxi any fears of an anti-climax were quickly diminished as the might and power of the architectural miracle that stood in front of us filled us with awe and admiration. The stature of the Giza pyramid was overwhelming with the immensity of its stones, making the construction of it so many centuries ago seem like a virtual impossibility. To truly appreciate all three pyramids and the historical changes around them we took a short camel ride in and around the desert, soaking in the natural views of the sand dunes on one side and the man-made views of the city on the other.

After a long, inspiring stay with the pyramids, we made our way to the Egyptian museum, where many historical artefacts still remain intact. We had already visited the tomb of Tutankhamen at the Valley of the Kings in Luxor and now we had the opportunity to look at the many treasures that were discovered in his tomb by the explorer Howard Carter. There were also several well-preserved mummies that lay at the centre of the museum, preserving the practices of the elite many hundreds of centuries ago.

Our stay in Cairo was short but packed with cultural and historical experiences that informed of us of an era where superstition and beliefs in various deities were common. As we prepared to leave the country, my heart sank at the thought of having to go back to the reality of life – a routine existence in an unpredictable climate with the same, familiar environment. At the same time, I felt utter gratefulness for having the opportunity to travel away from that mundane existence for a short time and experience a different world where my reality was temporarily forgotten.

Chapter Twenty-five

The Marriage game

The fun was over. It was time for my parents to start their search for the man of my dreams! Having experienced the process previously with my older siblings, my parents were now familiar with the market. They simply put the word out in to the community that their daughter required a husband. This community spread far beyond our locality: friends and relatives from all over the country were instructed to keep an eye out for possible candidates. My selling points were my education, my teaching career, my irrefutable past and my stable family background. Together with the declaration that I was now 'on the market', several conditions were also listed to try to sift out the unwanted. The possible candidate had to be educated, British and come from a reputable family. Once the word was out, we simply sat back and waited for the proposals to come flooding in.

I was nearly twenty-three when the search for my life partner began. Although to a Western eye this may seem young, from our cultural point of view, I was starting my search a little late. There was no guarantee of striking gold on the first hit: it could take months, or even years to come across a proposal where both parties gave the go ahead.

This serious business of marriage had to begin immediately!

Marrying a virtual stranger is a difficult concept to accept for those outside the faith. I feel indignation and shame at how my parents were forced to come together through a misguided system of culture and religion. With independence, education and support systems in place, the modern day Muslim women has the ability to empower herself if such situations arise, of which they do, be it a rare occurrence.

Although the reins of control for my marriage were firmly in my hands, it was difficult to imagine being able to make a decision about wanting to marry a man after just an hour of conversation. How would I be able to judge character and make a connection with someone I hardly knew? My older siblings seemed happy enough in their marriages, but the reality of their relationships were only known to them. Relationships between Muslim partners previous to their marriage was now commonplace, yet I had no experience of this phenomena, nor did my conscience ever allow me to pursue it. It was going to be a difficult, confusing journey, where my faith, friendships and family would all have to play a part in the decision making process.

Despite the apprehension, I did not question the concept of the modern day arranged marriage. From the moment I discovered the human desire to share one's life with another human being I knew that my parents would be the intermediaries. I was always bemused by the reaction I received from non-Muslim friends, who were shocked to discover that an independent, free-spirited woman like me would allow her parents to choose her life partner. They were tied by the stereotypical concept of forced marriages where the subservient woman bowed down to the demands of her family, unaware that this archaic concept was no longer a reality for most members of the Asian community. My explanation of the modern, truly Islamic arranged marriage put them at some ease, although the notion of developing a relationship after marriage still perplexed them.

The Messenger of Allah (sallallahu alayhi was sallam) said, "*When someone with whose religion and character you are satisfied asks to marry your daughter, comply with his request. If you do not do so, there will be corruption and great evil on earth.* " (Tirmidhi)

I was in agreement with my parents concerning the characteristics required for the potential suitor to get through our front door: family was important as the concept of 'marrying the family', at least from the girl's point of view, was still very much a reality. I accepted that I would initially have to share the same living space with my in-laws – an inherited cultural requirement from our ancestral Hindu culture that contradicts the Islamic perspective on living with the in-laws. There was a minority who were lucky enough to escape this claustrophobic way of living from the onset; however, I was far too realistic to have that expectation within me. I did however make the decision to make it clear during my 'interviews' with the potential spouses that I would not surrender to a lifetime of sharing my space with their family, giving them an approximate break off point of two years. Although it may seem clinical and impersonal to discuss such technicalities when you are looking for an emotional connection, they were to shape my future and therefore had a high priority in my list of requirements. My relationship with the in-laws could make or break the marriage and a clash of ideals between the two families could result in a problematic future so it was important that all expectations from both parties were made clear from the onset.

Imam al-Haskafi states in Durr al-Mukhtar: "*It is necessary for the husband to provide the wife with a shelter (home) that is free from his and her family members…. taking into consideration both their economic standings. A separate quarter within the house that has a lock, separate bathroom and kitchen will be (minimally) sufficient."*

The issue of an education, although not as rigid as the family background, was still an important factor. My dad had always made it clear to us how an education can shape one's perspective and understanding of life, building good character and providing the ability to look beyond the obvious. This is what I wanted in a life partner, and although I was not so naïve as to presume that a person could not be all of the above without an education, I was not prepared to take the risk when I would only have an hour to judge the character of the individual.

The next criterion that needed to be fulfilled was the requirement of a British passport. I strongly opposed the viewing of a potential husband from back home. Many 'visitors' who were looking for a means to remain in the UK permanently were roaming the marriage market, hoping to strike it lucky, but I wasn't even prepared to give them a look in! My ideal man spoke fluent English; he dressed with a sense of style and shared my same experiences of childhood and adolescence. I expected an instant, effortless connection, which I believed, was near impossible to achieve with a born and bred Indian.

One more condition that I put forward to my dad was the matter of where I was to live; the proposal could come from anywhere in the country as long as it wasn't in

Dewsbury! I had heard many stories of how the community in this tiny town were small-minded, backwards and overtly religious. Having lived in a relatively large town, I was also worried about settling in to a place where there was a lack of facilities for a full social life. I wanted my independence to continue and I was concerned that the town of Dewsbury may take this away from me.

Finally, there was the superficial matter of the external. All practicalities had to be ironed out in the initial interview between both suitors and the families so that there was no confusion in the future, however, without physical attraction, there was no future. I considered myself to be average looking: simple, plain but acceptable. With this in mind, I made the decision to follow my gut instinct. The little experience that I had with the science of physical chemistry gave me enough insight to sense when I was attracted to someone. I was now ready to begin the intrepid search for the man that would change the direction of my life forever.

Chapter Twenty-six

Potential Number One!

Someone had already picked up my status as a woman in search of a spouse and within a month, the first proposal arrived. Some more 'fatherly' fathers, when receiving such proposals, would initially interview the suitor themselves and judge their potential before handing them over to the daughter, however, my dad was very fond of his corner on the sofa, and so, as long as they fulfilled the criteria on paper, their first stop was with me.

The family parked their car outside our house. My sisters and I peered out of the net curtains upstairs, hoping to catch a glimpse of the star of the show. As they poured out in their best clothes we scrutinised each body until eventually the man of the moment revealed himself. Apart from the top of his head, we couldn't see much, but his build was to an acceptable standard: tall and lean without looking overly skinny. My first shot at the marriage game seemed to be going in the right direction and I was eager to see more.

We ran downstairs and waited in one of the front rooms. The men turned right into the room where my dad was waiting and the women walked into the room where my sisters and I were waiting; sitting with placidity and calm.

Everyone greeted each other, small talk was exchanged and shared acquaintances were identified. My grandma had a particular talent for drawing out common relatives from two families who barely knew each other so she was always invited to such occasions. As the women were politely nodding their heads they occasionally glimpsed at the three of us...curious to know who could potentially be joining their family but too polite to ask. Soon it was time for the guests to indulge in a cup of strong Indian tea and a plate full of savouries. This was the moment that the women had been waiting for. As I got up to collect their food from the kitchen all eyes turned towards me. At this point I was introduced as 'the girl' and the women finally had their chance to scrutinise me. I could feel their eyes screening me as I walked past them. I did get a sense of being objectified but at the same it was easy to accept as I was also making judgements about people I barely knew based on their appearances.

Once everyone was fully absorbed in the consumption of food and a busy exchange of mutual acquaintances I was told by my dad to make my way to my bedroom. This was where the interview was to take place. My younger sister and I shared the room so luckily there were two single beds – it would have been a little awkward sharing the same bed with a complete stranger! As I made myself comfortable sitting on one of the beds, taking deep breaths to calm the nerves, I heard my dad announce the words that I was to hear over and over again: "second on the left!" My first interviewee knocked on the door and let himself in.

We looked at each other, trying to disguise the significance of the moment. First impressions are an incredible tool, especially when one only has up to sixty minutes to judge the character of a person as well as deciphering whether there is any physical chemistry between you. His outward appearance was pleasant enough: his beauty didn't blow me away but at the same time I did not feel any repulsion, so this was a good start. We greeted each other with salutations of peace as is the Islamic way and I told him to take a seat on the bed opposite me. Then the questions began.

He was educated, had a good job and lived in Preston, just half an hour away from Bolton. So far, he was ticking all the boxes. When we talked about our shared faith, he gave me the impression that although he was a strong believer, he as yet had not been blessed with enough faith to pray the five daily prayers. At the time, this did not concern me as I was also lagging behind in my ability to practice my faith. Next there came the question that instantly set back the otherwise positive vibe of the interview. He asked me if I could drive – now if he had left it at that then that would have been a perfectly acceptable question, but he added that his mum and sister had asked him to ask me this question. His willingness to tell me that it was the females in his family that wanted to know if I was a driver gave me an insight in to how his mind was working and the expectations of his mother and sister. A question such as this should have been at the bottom of his list of priorities: I had no intention to be the chauffeur of the family, or at least not to be told indirectly that this was to be one of my roles once I was part of the family in the first interview! Surely common sense should have made my interviewee realise this, but clearly he lacked the intelligence to omit his female relatives from the question. My presumptions may seem harsh and perhaps misguided, but it was essential that I erred on the side of precaution to ensure that I was not being chosen for my ability to please his family more than my ability to please him. Our culture was such that sometimes men put their families before their wives and I had no intention of being secondary to a mother and sister.

Prophet Muhammad (sallallahu alayhi was sallam) said, *"The believer with the most complete faith is the one with the best character, and the best of them are those whom treat their women the best."* (Tirmidhi)

His previous question had left a negative imprint in my subconscious and no matter how hard I tried to brush it away the feeling of uneasiness and doubt would not go away. Our interview continued for several more minutes but my enthusiasm dwindled as I made the firm decision in my mind that this was not the marriage for me.

As soon as a moment of silence came to pass I politely suggested that maybe we should end the interview now. As he left my bedroom I felt relief that my first experience of an arranged marriage meeting was over and grateful that I knew exactly what I was to say to my parents. It was not customary for the girl and boy to discuss their feelings about the interview with each other – each party was given a little time to consider their position, after which the girl's family would contact the boy's family through their intermediary with a response of a firm yes or no or a maybe, in which case a second meeting is arranged.

I waited in my bedroom till I saw the family leave. Then, I made the first of many descents down to the living room where my parents were waiting in anticipation, praying for a pleasing response. However, the expression on my face gave them a clear indication of my feelings as I nodded my head in the negative. They let out a short sigh of disappointment then inquired as to what it was that allowed me to make my mind up so quickly. Knowing that my parents would consider the 'chauffeur' issue as petty and insignificant, I responded with the standard excuses: a lack of chemistry; awkward silences; stilted conversation and a general mismatch of personalities.

The Messenger of Allah (sallallahu alayhi was sallam) said, *"A woman whom has been previously married has more right concerning herself than her guardian, and a virgin's consent must be asked about herself…"* (Bukhari and Muslim)

As this was my first interview, my parents accepted my excuses, comforted by the fact that there was still time and plenty of potential proposals in the pipeline. They would inform the intermediary of my decision and that would be an end to the matter. We would never find out the standpoint of the boy and his family as once they received a reply in the negative, the proposal was no longer allowed to be pursued.

We brushed off the last of the samosas that were left over by our guests and laughed about how many more plates of savouries we would have to serve to perfectly good strangers before we would finally find the right match.

A steady flow of proposals continued to grace our home and 'second on the left' became a regular utterance at the bottom of the stairs. I rejected many of the men that came to see me and, although we never discovered their perspective on the meetings, they could have just as easily rejected me too. My parent's disappointed expressions as I gave them my decision in the negative were getting more extreme and their sighs of desperation were becoming difficult to bear. Although they never pressured me directly, I could sense the strain they were under as the need to marry off their now twenty four year old daughter was becoming a matter of urgency.

There were a handful of men out of the approximate twenty five that I had interviewed so far in the space of two years that I didn't reject, however, for reasons I never discovered, they rejected me. The list of possible reasons that swayed them towards the negative could have been one of many: my desire to remain in full time work after marriage; an unwillingness to remain living in the same house with his family long term; not matching their ideal of figure and beauty or the reason that was most common in my list of rejections – a lack of chemistry and natural flow of conversation where we simply didn't click.

I recognised that mutual chemistry became easier with experience. Within a few minutes I would be able to judge whether the man sitting in front of me was a definite no or a possibility. An instant ability to make conversation was always a good sign, although the content of that conversation could sway me either way. Laughter was also an indication that I could be heading towards a relationship: the situation of two strangers meeting in a bedroom with their families eagerly waiting for the outcome downstairs was an awkward one, so being able to get through this with laughter, banter and a little flirtation was always a happy starting point.

Chapter Twenty-seven

Unwanted baggage

Occasionally, the interview would be held at the boy's house. We were now tired of frying savouries and making cups of Indian tea so this was often a welcome break! A couple of members of my family, usually my younger sister and mum, and I, would go to the house as guests and when it was time for the interview I would be shown to the room where the boy would be waiting. One such occasion was a proposal from within Bolton. We knew the family had a good reputation, and although I had never met the boy before, we had high hopes that perhaps this could be the one.

I walked in to his front room where he was waiting. On a purely physical level I was impressed immediately! He was tall and handsome with fair skin and light eyes: an attractive combination. His impressive exterior instantly prodded at my own insecurities about my appearance: I was also tall, but just a little too skinny with an unimpressive boyish figure and my bland facial features were nothing to write home about. Nevertheless, I decided that I would make the most of the pleasant view by indulging in a long interview, despite knowing that the most likely outcome was going to be rejection.

Despite this being his first official marriage interview our conversation flowed naturally. We laughed together and even indulged in a little flirtation. Things seemed to be going extremely well but I refused to allow hope to enter in to my heart: this one hour of joviality was exactly that. I refused to be analytical about the meeting afterwards – there was no point until I received an answer from him (it was his right to answer first as we had the meeting in his house). So afterwards, I shared my interpretation of the interview with my parents: that he was extremely good looking therefore highly reducing the possibility of a match however, we seemed to be enjoying each other's company so there was a very slight possibility that we could be taking the next step.

After a few days, when all thoughts of my latest, handsome proposal had left my mind, we received an unexpected call: he wanted to meet me for a second time! Apparently, he was happy with the way our interview went and wished to see me again so that he could discuss some important matter that he had not revealed in the first interview. I was surprised but intrigued as to what this 'important matter' could be so I agreed to another encounter in his front room. My parents were more than willing for me to take this next step: it was one step closer to their goal of 'marrying off' their second daughter who seemed to be dragging her feet when it came to selecting the man of her dreams.

Without any expectations I made my way through the door of the front room a second time. Conversation began to flow again, and just as I was beginning to enjoy myself, he abruptly reminded me that he had called me over for a specific reason. Choosing his words carefully, he began to explain his past deeds and the consequences of his wayward behaviour.

He confessed to being a father of a five year old boy, having had a relationship with a white girl when he was younger. Details of a rebellious past poured out as he tried to show the sincerity of his regret. Next, he moved on to the present situation that he found himself in: he wanted to marry a Muslim girl, but a Muslim girl that was willing to undertake sharing the responsibility of a five year old boy. He was not happy with his son's non-religious upbringing and wished to fight for sufficient custody so that his son could be bought up with some Islamic values and traditions. Finally, he apologised for not revealing this vital information previously – he had to have the initial interview to firstly judge if we had chemistry and secondly to decide if I was a person able to at least listen to his confession without making harsh, critical judgements.

So now, it was my turn to speak. As he was talking, I

had the opportunity to absorb the shock of hearing a confession on such a grand scale. By the time the confession ended I had already made up my mind. I had no emotional attachment to this man, no promises had been made and we had not undertaken any verbal or handshake agreements. If the confession excluded the existence of a child, then I could have considered the proposal, as we truly did have chemistry between us, but this declaration of evidence from his past only served to confirm my decision.

The insecure cynic within me also questioned why he had chosen to reveal his murky past to me, the plain Jane, in comparison to his well chiselled finery. Did he think I was a pushover and that I would be bought to my knees by his impeccable good looks? Would I say yes out of desperation having seen so many prospects without success already? Such unwarranted thoughts were not going to be a good basis to start a relationship!

And so, I let him down gently. There was no point of leaving him hanging, and from the expression on his face, I sensed that he already knew what my response was going to be. I felt sorry for him. Circumstances and bad choices together with immaturity had landed him in a difficult situation; however, I was not the one to provide him with the answers.

As I gave him the reasons as to why I would have to reject the proposal, he nodded his head in agreement, looking painfully sad, not just because of my words, but by the thought of what difficulties he might face in the future. I wished him good luck, told him I would pray that Allah will give him the wife that he was looking for and promised him that I would keep his secret safely within the family.

My parents were also shocked to hear about the child. They were even more shocked that nobody in the community was aware of the boy's past, as usually such information was readily available, especially when an investigation is conducted prior to accepting a prospective proposal. We decided to answer with a generic 'lack of chemistry' to those enquiring about the proposal outside the family and kept the real reason secret.

The experience of this particular proposal was a learning curve for me. I knew that our culture was infusing with the West, and that morals were declining, but I got to see first-hand the consequences of the past haunting a person who wants to move on and escape their previous life to live a more pious, God-fearing existence. With true repentance, if Allah wills, every type of regret can be forgiven:

On the authority of Anas, who said: I heard the messenger of Allah say:

Allah the Almighty has said: "*O son of Adam, so long as you call upon Me and ask of Me, I shall forgive you for what you have done, and I shall not mind. O son of Adam, were your sins to reach the clouds of the sky and were you then to ask forgiveness of Me, I would forgive you. O son of Adam, were you to come to Me with sins nearly as great as the earth and were you then to face Me, ascribing no partner to Me, I would bring you forgiveness nearly as great as its."* {Tirmidhi}

Chapter Twenty-eight

A Sneaked-in Indian

It was clear that my parents were getting desperate – so desperate in fact that they were willing to sneak an Indian in to my bedroom whilst I was out, hence leaving me with no choice on my return but to chat with the man from back home who was awkwardly awaiting the arrival of his possible bride.

I was at my friend's house round the corner when the carefully planned meeting took place. A family friend had bought the proposal forward, and knowing that I would dismiss it straight away my dad and his friend had decided to keep it from me. Whilst at my friend's home I received a call from my dad asking me to come back home as he needed my help with an urgent matter. When I walked through the door my dad and his friend were sitting on the front room couch with huge grins on their faces. They told me of the immigrant hiding in my bedroom and asked me to go upstairs and have a polite, open minded conversation with him. I was struck with utter disbelief...not about the fact that the boy was an Indian, but about the fact that my dad and his friend were capable of setting up such an encounter without giving even a slight indication of their intentions.

I felt sorry for the poor soul who was sat upstairs unaware of the way he was being used as a pawn in my dad's game, so I reluctantly made my way upstairs - but not before I told my dad in no uncertain terms that the possibility of success was an absolute zero.

As I have said before, first impressions linger: he looked smart, but more geeky than trendy; his hair was styled, but it consisted of a side parting and an over-indulgent use of oil; he spoke English, but with limited vocabulary. Our conversation was short and awkward, despite his degree in sociology that he had completed in India. Whether it was my stubborn refusal to see beyond the 'Indian-ness' that didn't allow the conversation to flow or my many pre-conceptions of the typical man from back home, I knew without any doubt that the interview was a complete failure.

As he left the room, I felt a small pang of guilt. He had come to my house blissfully unaware that I had no intention to even consider his proposal. My dad had used him to trick me in to a conversation with the one type of man that I refused to see. The justification behind the treachery was that I would at least consider the possibility of an Indian husband, however, my dad clearly made the wrong choice when it came to selecting the guinea pig for his little experiment: I wanted chemistry, good vibes and shared experiences – something which I believed was near impossible to achieve with an Indian.

Many more proposals came and went. One had only come to see me to ease the pressure he was under from his parents: as I was about to make my way up to my bedroom for our official chat, my brother whispered in my ear that he already had a long term girlfriend…so that was another waste of perfectly good samosas and kebabs!

Others were passable in personality, but far too short. Some were good to talk to, but their immaturity was off putting. A few lacked any sense of ambition whilst the odd one, as cruel as it sounds, was not very pleasing on the eye. It was now approaching three long years of husband hunting and we were all becoming impatient. My parents tried not to show the worry and pressure that they were under, but each time a proposal failed, their fears increased. No parent wanted their daughter sitting at home, single and without the possibility of having a family of her own. I was also now desperate to find the man for me, but in the meantime I was consoled by my faith in finding patience and accepting that my destined partner was waiting for me out there in the big wide world: it was only a matter of time.

Chapter Twenty-nine

The last escape

I had now reached the point where I had lost count of how many strange men I had entertained in my bedroom! The stress of the situation was beginning to takes its toll on everyone, so when my close friend Saliha suggested that the two of us go away on a girlie holiday; it seemed like the perfect temporary solution.

I found it much easier to pluck up the courage to ask this time, having already treaded the path granting permission to take a trip abroad. My dad was quick to answer in the positive, so without hesitation, we went ahead and booked a week in Barcelona.

I felt privileged as a 24 year old single woman out to enjoy new experiences in an exciting city with one of my closest friends: I couldn't wait to taste the tapas, soak in the culture, admire the architecture and consort with the locals. Our hotel was situated in the centre of Barcelona on the famous Las Ramblas – a long walkway offering countless tapas bars and restaurants, with street entertainment and plenty of shopping opportunities.

During the day, with our sun lotion at the ready, we would use our guide book to explore the history of Barcelona. The Sagrada Familia – a cathedral like building designed by the famous Spanish architect Gaudi, impressed us. His work was evident all around Barcelona, giving the city its unique character.

We also took leisurely walks around the old town, making our way through narrow streets and alleyways. The Museu Piccaso told of the life of the famous artist and we were able to view several of his original works of art. We also visited the Olympic stadium, taking a walk around the grounds and trying to imagine the incredible atmosphere that must have resonated all around the stadium in 1992.

Our trip to the beach was a memorable one: I hadn't worn a swimming costume since the forgettable days of P.E at high school, yet here I was on a beach, ready to bare all – except of course my concept of baring all was showing a bit of arm and leg! Despite my knee length shorts and vest top I found it extremely difficult to relax. The beach itself was beautiful – clean, yellow sands and soft, soothing waves, but I sat huddled on the edge of the water for quite some time.

Eventually, I loosened up a little and began to wade at the edge of the Mediterranean Sea. As we were chatting and savouring the freedom of the water, we noticed an Indian/Pakistani looking man bobbing up and down in the water a few metres away from us. He was blatantly staring at the two of us, hedging his bets on the fact that we shared the same skin colour. But despite our best efforts to avoid eye contact, his persistent and almost obsessive stare only served to freak us out. We promptly left the beach, dressing ourselves inside a towel to avoid the stare of any lurking peeping toms.

We had the pleasure of encountering another short term stalker who looked to be of the Indian/Pakistani variety whilst walking along Las Ramblas one evening. He seemed to think that we wouldn't notice if he had his head in a newspaper, but this only made us giggle, as he was playing into the most stereotypical, almost cartoon like concept of how a stalker behaves! We felt perfectly safe as there were hundreds of people around us, yet this man was getting some sort of cheap thrill by following us in his unprofessional capacity as an amateur stalker.

Eventually we got tired of stopping off at postcards stands to see if he would continue to follow us. We saw a local policeman and quickly pointed the stalker out. This made the stalker walk in the opposite direction with full speed and his manner of getting kicks came to an abrupt end.

During the evenings and into the night, we would select a restaurant and take our time in choosing from the varied menu. Then we would take our time to eat, watching passers-by and making conversation with other tourists. During one of these evenings we met three lads from Nottingham. They came across to where we were sitting and asked to join us: we happily obliged. The conversation was easy, especially after we discovered that all five of us had one thing in common: we were all in the marriage market and our parents were desperately searching for our potential spouses. This served to strengthen our bond, although two of them, Chander and Sahib, were of the Sikh faith, so the possibility of a match between us was an absolute impossibility.

The other lad who was Muslim was reasonably attractive, but he didn't seem to warm to our company. It seemed that our intrusion in to his evening was restricting the possibilities that would otherwise be open to him – he had to demonstrate respect in front of his fellow 'sisters' and so, was required to keep a handle on whatever it was that he would otherwise have indulged in.

The whole night was full of laughter and stories, and so, we decided to meet up the next day for an excursion to Montserrat – a monk monastery situated an hour away by train and set amongst the breath-taking scenery of mountains and rock formations.

The day at Montserrat was one of the most memorable in my life. As well as the incredible scenery, I felt utterly happy and truly entertained. Chander managed to captivate the passengers of the whole cable car, which was taking us up to the monk's retreat, with his witty charm and humour. His charismatic personality was infectious and hugely attractive, drawing in the crowds wherever he went.

Throughout the day we shared our comments about the beautiful surroundings and relaxed in the sun, taking posy pictures of each other at every opportunity. The most enjoyable poses were the ones where all of us looked away from the lens with a thoughtful expression on our faces in different directions. It was an attempt to create a more artistic, meaningful picture, however confusing it might have been for the bemused passer-by who we elected to click the camera!

Just as we began making our descent on foot, we came across an abandoned café hidden amongst the tops of the mountains. Inside there was shattered glass and turned up tables scattered across the floor, but as we walked onto the extensive balcony, we were met with incredible views – and five, perfectly good chairs just waiting to be sat on. As we relaxed and lost ourselves in our own private thoughts, Chander began to click his camera, likening himself to a professional. Thankfully, the pictures that he took were impressive, and his framed wedding gift still hangs proudly on my wall as a reminder of that perfect moment in the mountains of Montserrat.

The boys were leaving two days after our excursion, so we decided to meet one more time for a meal in the evening. Again, banter and witty conversation flowed throughout the evening. I was completely taken in by Chander's sense of humour, but I knew that every person who met him was also drawn in by his charm, so I did not allow my feelings to progress any further. There was also the complication of our different faiths, which was an immovable barrier for both of us, and also of course, the necessity of mutual attraction.

After exchanging numbers, and promising to meet up back home, the boys left and we continued with our holiday, making the most of every moment. We not only had to go back home and face the reality of life that every holiday maker dreads, but there was also the little matter of finding a husband!

As much as we prayed for it to stand still, time flew by. We said goodbye to the guaranteed scorching temperatures and laid back lifestyle, preparing ourselves in re-joining the rat race. Forty eight hours after we said goodbye to our British friends in Barcelona, we were back in the UK. Saliha and I returned to our homes, appreciating the fact that we still had a couple of weeks of the summer holiday left before we would have to return to work.

It was within those two weeks that Chander got in touch, wanting to organise a re-union. Although it hadn't been long since we last saw them, Saliha and I thought the timing was perfect, as once back in to work, the re-union would have been much more difficult to organise.

So there we were again: sitting in a café in Nottingham with conversation in full flow. The tapas was missing, as was the Mediterranean sun, but the buzz was still there. Chander was as entertaining as ever: his ability to bring humour in to the conversation without coming across as arrogant or self-absorbed was a credit to his gentle nature.

We spent the day walking around the centre of Nottingham, ending it with an evening meal at a restaurant. At one point, Chander and I found ourselves on our own and it was then that we had a conversation, which was extremely flattering, but also demonstrated our maturity when it came to understanding relationships.

It was clear to me how I felt about him, but he now returned the compliment by telling me that he harboured some feelings towards me. There was always a spark between the two of us, but I remained cautious not to interpret this chemistry as anything other than friendship, however, it now seemed that my gut instinct hadn't let me down.

After sharing our mutual admiration and attraction for each other we continued to discuss how the prospect of a relationship was impossible. We both knew that our individual faiths were of the upmost importance. It dictated our thoughts and choices so, for a successful marriage, we had to have partners of the same faith. We were also very realistic about the importance of family background and expectations. Within a short space of time, we concluded that our mutual attraction was of no benefit in the long run and therefore pointless to pursue.

It was an easy conversation in terms of spoken words, but the hurt was still there. Chander was the man of my dreams – he ticked all of the boxes apart from the one dearest to my heart. Without the sharing of the same faith my conscience would have been in constant battle, and once the novelty of the relationship wore off, we would have struggled to cope with our own sense of spirituality as well as the practicalities of the marriage.

As the others returned, we ended our discussion with a mutual respect and understanding of each other. Our day of reminiscing had ended and it was time to say good bye for the second time. Hugs were exchanged and promises of keeping in touch were made. The extra-long hug between Chander and I raised some friendly suspicion with Saliha, but as I explained to her later, any thoughts of pursuing the relationship would only complicate our lives, stalling our search for the right partner.

We did keep in touch for a while. Chander and Sahib even made the effort to hand-deliver our framed wedding presents to our doors. Unfortunately, neither Saliha nor I were at home when they made their impromptu visit so the last time I saw Chander was at our re-union in Nottingham. The last I heard of the boys was several years ago when they were all married, having completed the intrepid journey of searching for a spouse.

The experiences and people that I met in Barcelona confirmed my maturity and strengthened my faith. My love for my faith and my trust in Allah withheld my temporary desires, hence protecting me from the pain and anguish of an impossible relationship. It was an easy decision: putting Allah first; and I thanked Him for giving me the insight to do this.

It may be that you hate something when it is good for you and it may be that you love something when it is bad for you. Allah knows and you do not know.   Quran (Surat al-Baqara: 216)

A non-believer who might be reading this book might consider my thought processes futile. Who is missing out from an exciting, unpredictable adventure by giving up a relationship before it has even begun? Isn't all this soul searching and guilt destroying my freedom? Yet, because of my absolute belief in the existence of a merciful God and my complete trust in Him, such decisions are simple to make. If faith is weak, then life can become a struggle of two minds, but when faith is strong, there is an implicit belief in the words of Allah and true, long lasting happiness comes from striving to do all it takes to please Him.

When God intends goodness for someone, He opens the door of humility, perpetual search for refuge and dependence upon Him. He opens the door where the self's faults, ignorance and enmity are sighted; where blessings of its Lord, His excellence, mercy, and generosity are witnessed – the door of His goodness, wealth and praise. (P4, The invocation of God by Ibn Qayyim al-Jawziyya)

Chapter Thirty

Good things come to those who wait...

Although my faith influenced the decisions I made in my life, as yet I had not discovered the miraculous nature and power of prayer. I would talk to Allah and ask him for guidance, but my inconsistency of the required five daily prayers meant I often lacked a deep spirituality in my manner of supplication. However, even without an absolute devoutness, reaching out to Allah gave me an overwhelming sense of peace. The notion of divine destiny asks of the believer to strive in reaching their goal and then to accept the outcome as the divine ruling of Allah. This also helped me to accept that I would meet my life partner only when it was my destiny to do so.

I was now somewhere in the thirties concerning the number of proposals I had interviewed and my dad was ready to add to that number with another prospect. He had already agreed with the intermediary that the meeting would go ahead, but as he listed the credentials of the interviewee, my hope for any possible match faded.

Firstly, he was from Dewsbury: the one place that I had set my heart against and secondly, he originated from India. My dad insisted that the fact that he was not British-born would not be an issue as he had already inhabited the

UK for several years. He also spoke fluent English and dressed with just as much style as my British counterparts. My dad had gained this precious insider information because, for the first time since the search for his second son-in-law had begun, he had undertaken a pre-interview with the said candidate. By now, my dad had a definite idea as to what constituted an absolute rejection on my part, so I allowed myself to trust his judgement concerning the issue of background.

However, there was still the matter of settling in Dewsbury. Although I would not judge a person simply by their town of habitation, I was to possibly spend the rest of my life there, so making my feelings clear from the onset was a sensible move. Again, my dad attempted to quash my worries when he claimed that the boy would happily move to Bolton.

I was not convinced, but as my dad had taken the time and trouble to pre-assess the potential of this boy, I told him that I would go ahead with the interview, reminding him of the very likely possibility that this would be yet another disappointment.

After the familiar 'second on the left', came the knock on the door, followed by my first look at the potential reject. However, his reject status was quickly promoted to a possible maybe when my pre-conceptions were given a harsh slap in the face: I found myself impressed with what walked through the door. He wore smart, perfect fit jeans and a black, ribbed jumper. His hair was styled in a contemporary fashion and he carried an air of confidence. As we greeted each other and began the familiar spiel of family, education, religion and our hopes for the future, I secretly admired his ability to speak fluent English, be it with a hint of Indian.

The content of his conversation was also making a good impression: he seemed ambitious, far more than many of the British prospects I had interviewed. Since arriving in England he had entered in to the education system and had completed a HND in ICT as well as attaining an adult teaching certificate. He was now teaching this subject to mature students at a local college.

His mum and now late father had arrived in the UK in the same period as my own parents, so his younger brother and sister were both British born. This led to the question about why he was born and raised in India. Although he did not go in to much detail, he told me that his mum had to leave him in India when he was one and come to the UK. Until the age of eighteen, which was when he first arrived in England, his grandparents raised him. Once in the UK, via a student visa, he lived with his 'new' family in Dewsbury.

I was happy with this response for now. Investigations in to the family background were my dad's responsibility:

my duty was to find a genuine connection with the man in front of me, to find common ground and to feel a chemistry that could be the beginnings of a beautiful relationship.

The requirement of flowing conversation had been fulfilled. We were relaxed and comfortable in each other's company. I breached the subject of where we were to live if the interview was successful and just as I had suspected, he knew nothing of the condition that my dad had attempted to reassure me with of settling in Bolton. Leaving this aside, I announced my own condition of intending to live with his family for a set period of time, rather than a life-time and also made it clear that I intended to work after marriage.

He listened and nodded his head in agreement. If any of my requirements were not suitable to him or his family, he had the opportunity to decline the proposal, even if I was to accept. We continued to discuss practicalities, with some humorous banter in-between for light relief. I was happy with the way things were going and I got the impression that he was too. Soon, we heard a knock on the door signalling that our time was up, so we said our goodbyes and once again, I found myself in a position where my life could be transformed by the utterance of a simple yes.

As I waited for him to leave the house I considered my decision whilst my parents waited downstairs, praying and hoping that I would not miss yet another opportunity of marriage. When I heard the front door close I walked down the stairs, turned the corner and was met with my parents eagerly anticipating stares. As I nodded in the affirmative, much to their surprise, I swear I could see the creases on their foreheads soften as they unburdened themselves with the years of built up stress!

I reminded them that their relief was a little premature as their 'son-in-law' had only just walked out of the front door, but they seemed sure that the fact that he had not yet achieved British citizenship would heavily influence the decision. I was also aware that his first reason in agreeing to marry me could be pressure from the family, but judging from his confidence and independence, and the fact that he had seen several girls before me, suggested that he was capable of setting aside the pressures of obtaining a red passport to ensure that he married the girl that was right for him. Whatever the motivation and outcome, I was happy with my decision. My instincts and experience in searching for a spouse told me that there was no reason to turn this one down and so, we made the decision to accept the proposal. Now all we had to do was wait for his response.

We didn't have long to wait: the next day…the man from Dewsbury…he said yes!

The long search for my life partner had finally come to an end. There was all round relief and some cautious celebration as we allowed ourselves to enjoy the moment. His name was Arif: the man that I had only spent one hour with was now the man I was to spend the rest of my life with. Experience had taught me to feel comfortable with that thought. From the onset, we both knew that we would have to make a life-long decision in a short space of time. We were both committed to the concept of marriage and were determined to make it work before it even began. This was how arranged marriages worked: families, expectations, ambitions, life styles, financial standing, careers, religion and physical attraction – these were all discussed, assessed and judged. Once these qualities were matched, it was up to the couple to make their relationship work and, because of the sanctity of marriage and the commitment made in front of God, both parties would put their heart and soul in to making the marriage a success.

"Allah, Most High, says in The Holy Quran
Among His signs is [the fact] that He has created spouses for you among yourselves so that you may dwell in tranquillity with them, and He has planted love and mercy between you. In that are signs for people who reflect [Quran 30.21]

The official meeting of families was arranged to discuss dates and to begin the process of familiarisation. Arif's family had not come to the initial meeting, so as yet I had not met his parents or his siblings, although the two dads had met previously. Within a matter of days I found myself sitting on the carpet of our front living room with my sisters and cousins. Arif's female relatives were sat around us on the sofas. I overheard one of his auntie's asking my future mother-in-law which one of us was to join their family, and as my mother-in-law had no idea, I quickly obliged by putting my hand up and declaring that I was the one they were curious to see. My lack of inhibition, which was unheard of in their generation, put a smile on their faces and set a standard that I continued to display in all future in-law gatherings.

It was decided that in three weeks time we were to have a small engagement ceremony at my house as well as our Nikah (declaration of religious vows). The Nikah would make our marriage official, enabling the two of us to meet on our own whilst staying within the boundaries of Islam as well as adhering to cultural expectations.

I was comfortable with this time scale as my concept of marriage was not based upon the Western norm of meeting someone, falling in love and eventually getting married. Arranged marriages began with commitment, and love would hopefully follow. I strongly believed that pleasing Allah and remaining faithful to His commandments would set me up for a happy, inspiring relationship: love would grow as long as we nurtured our partnership into a relationship where mutual respect, honesty, patience and compromise were honoured.

The partnership was ready, and it was now time to put our non-existent relationship in to overdrive. We had three weeks to learn all we could about each other and to develop a connection that was based on more than just practicalities. I asked my dad to get Arif's mobile number so that the journey to find the mutual love could begin.

Our first communication was to arrange a date so that we could talk face to face one more time before our engagement. Both families were so elated by the union that they allowed us to meet without a chaperone. We met at Frankie and Benny's in Bolton, four days after we had spoken for the first time in my bedroom. I was nervous, concerned that doubt may creep in after a second look, but fortunately, the date only confirmed what I had already decided. My heart was at peace and my body was satisfied with the chemistry that was beginning to stir inside me. Finally, I got the man that I wanted.

For the next two weeks, Arif and I spent hours on the phone every evening talking, laughing and sometimes sharing silence. We exchanged meaningful text messages on our Nokia phones and tried our upmost to learn all we could about each other's lives.

The date of the engagement/Nikah soon arrived. Guests

rolled in as I sat in our cleared out living room, dressed to impress, waiting for my fiancée to join me. It was at this point that I realised that I could not remember what Arif looked like! There I was, dressed in an elegant Indian outfit with stunning hair and make-up, looking the best that I had ever looked in my life, yet I could not recall the face of the man for whom all this prettification was intended.

As I was telling my best friends this remarkable fact, I saw a group of boys outside the front door making their way into the house. Thankfully, one of them carried a beautiful bouquet of red roses, so I presumed that whoever handed me the roses was my fiancée! Arif walked in to the room first with the bouquet in his hand. At this point, my memory burst in to life and confirmed that he was indeed the man that I had agreed to marry! Seeing him after so many hours of conversation on the phone brought with it a rush of excitement. I couldn't wait to be on my own with him as I now felt that I knew him so much better than our first meeting.

Cameras clicked as he handed over the bouquet and complimented me on the way I looked. Despite the many pairs of eyes scrutinising our compatibility, I felt that we were sharing a very private moment together. That first look in to each other's eyes was a declaration of our commitment to each other and an exchange of emotions that told of the bliss that we were experiencing.

After half an hour of banter between the guests and us, it was time for the Nikah. Islamic marriage vows are declared separately, so Arif went to the local mosque and I stayed at home. We were reminded about the sanctity of marriage by the imams of the mosque, with two witnesses present, and then asked three times if we were happy to marry our partner. We replied with a simple yes, and then we signed a Nikah certificate, all as separate parties.

The Qur'an says:

"Your wives are a garment for you, and you are a garment for them." (2:187)

"It is He who created you from a single soul, And made its mate of like nature in order that you might dwell with her in love." (7:189)

Once the short religious ceremony was over, and we were declared husband and wife, we were re-united as a married couple. Congratulations and hugs were exchanged as the camera continued to click at every opportunity: family portraits, exchanging of rings and confetti moments were all captured as high spirits continued to run through the occasion.

By the evening, the guests had dwindled and the celebratory atmosphere had gone. After hours of sharing, I finally had the opportunity to spend some time on my own with Arif. I knew that if we stayed in the house, we would not get the privacy I was looking for, so we jumped in to Arif's car and drove to my favourite spot on the outskirts of Bolton, Rivington, where I had spent many sunny days enjoying the scenery and exploring the surroundings with my friends. We drove up to the highest point of the area, and although it was a cold, dark evening in the middle of November, I was determined to make this moment as romantic and memorable as possible.

The moment lived up to its expectations. Our first affectionate touch was full of romance and what made it even more beautiful was the fact that we were now committed to each other for life. We had recited our marriage vows after only meeting face to face twice yet, thanks to the blessings of Allah; I was truly at ease with the future and felt an inner calm and peace when I was with the man who was now my husband.

We now had six months of bliss before we were to have the big wedding ceremony that would dramatically change my life in terms of where I lived, where I worked and with whom I socialized. However, I didn't allow this forthcoming reality to cloud my view of the immediate future: I was to spend six heavenly months indulging in a carefree life where I had the comfort and security of my own home, family and friends and a long distance husband who took me out every weekend on perfect dates. Life was wonderful.

If however, the process let me down, I always had the difficult option of backing out. Everything on paper was satisfactory and Arif's personality was becoming increasingly attractive as I got to know him, but sometimes nasty surprises can be lurking around the corner and they only show themselves further down the relationship line. If this was the case, then I would have to be strong and back out of the marriage before it became physical, which most Islamically united couples waited for, until after the marriage ceremony. It was always a last resort, with many consequences, but my parent's turbulent, and for the most part, unhappy relationship had taught me the importance of compatibility and the absolute need for mutual respect.

The Quran says:

If a wife fears cruelty or desertion on her husband's part, there is no blame on them if they arrange an amicable settlement between themselves;...
- Surah 4 Verse 128

Sunan of Abu-Dawood Hadith 2173   Narrated   by Abdullah ibn Umar

The Prophet (saws) said: *'Of all the lawful acts' the most detestable to Allah is divorce.'*

The Islamic scholars agree that if the one who initiates the divorce in their marriage is confident that they will be able to justify the reasons for initiating the divorce in the Presence of Allah on the Day of Judgment, and they are confident that their Lord will accept their excuse then all such reasons would be deemed valid grounds for divorce.

Alhamdulillah (All praises to Allah), I never felt even a twitch of doubt throughout our six months of dating. Sometimes I would waste time thinking about our differences: I would tell a joke, or make a sarcastic remark, but his inexperience of English humour would result in a rather confused response. When talking about my childhood memories, such as re-enacting Wham videos or eating crushed up thingies, he would listen without sharing the nostalgia. However, it didn't take me long to realise that he also had many childhood stories to share and his tales of memories past were far more interesting than mine!

I spent the next six months with my head in the clouds. It was without doubt one of the happiest periods of my life: my home life was bordering normality; my older brother's wife had just given birth to a baby girl, making me an auntie for the second time and my parents were content that they had now found spouses for three out of their five children.

Throughout those six months, I never took the time to seriously think about how my life would change once I was married. I was looking at life through rose-tinted glasses, giving thought only to the joy of spending more time with Arif. At the time, I did not consider the pressures of sharing the same living space with a new family – a family that was already established - where I would be the stranger who would have to adjust and compromise to ensure that I was accepted.

So without any serious consideration about the reality of my future, I began to prepare for my elaborate wedding day. My only concerns were my bridal outfit, the decoration of the stage and the wedding cake. The venue, the majority of the guests and the food were all decided upon and organised by my dad.

Over one thousand people were invited – most of whom I considered to be complete strangers. My parents were obliged to invite all the families that had a link with their villages of origin back in India – any overlooked guests would take serious offence, so guests were traced from all over the country. The venue was a large hall on the first floor of the mosque and the food consisted of oversized pots full to the brim with white rice and dhal.

Arif and I spent most of our big day sitting on ornate chairs on an elaborately decorated stage. Guests came up to congratulate us and take pictures. Some shook our hands whilst others hugged us: the older generation of women would stroke our hair and faces affectionately, saying prayers for our future happiness, but all I could think about was my expensive hair and make-up being ruined! It was a long day, and although it was exciting to be the centre of attention, all Arif and I could think about was escaping the colourful crowds so that we could be on our own.

At five o clock in the afternoon the main events of the day had been ticked off the list: the feeding frenzy was over; gifts had been exchanged; family photographs had been taken and the wedding cake had been cut. There was only one formality left: the official handing over of the bride to the new family.

This was always an emotional part of all weddings. Arif left the stage and my female relatives joined me. My head and face were covered with a red bridal shawl and a religious song, with lyrics that told of how a daughter must leave her home, was played in the background. There was silence from the guests as they watched the emotional drama unfold and as soon as the tears started flowing on stage, the guests also started to weep as they became emotionally involved in the spectacle before them.

The hugs and prayers continued as I was led off the stage. Arif's family now became part of the poignant drama as they assured my family with clichés such as: they would treat me like a daughter of their own and that they had nothing to worry about as I would be taken care of so well that I would never miss my home or family. Eventually, I was out of the building. The people around me moved aside as I said an emotional farewell to my dad. I still remember seeing my dad out of the corner of my eye, leaning against a wall, sobbing, as I climbed in to Arif's car.

The manner of saying farewell may seem a little melodramatic, after all, I was only moving an hour's drive away across the M62, but for a daughter, marriage changed everything. There were unwritten rules that I had to adhere to: my loyalties would now have to lie with my husband's parents; I would have to seek their approval with certain decisions that I made; the number of times I visited my parents would have to be restricted and, although my in-laws never verbally expressed these expectations of me, I knew I had to hold back on expressing my opinions on certain matters and remain respectful, even if I felt that I was not in the wrong. The freedom that I had taken for granted at my parent's home was now going to have to be compromised and it was the loss of this independence and the transition into a more mature life style that was being mourned.

However, there is no crystal ball that predicts our future and so dwelling on what might be was futile. I left the fear of change in the hands of God, trusting Him to help me with what lay ahead, and looked forward to the immediate future.

Within two minutes of sitting in Arif's car, my tears had dried up: it was time to start living my married life. As my family followed the tradition of physically blocking the wedding car, not moving until Arif presented them with a substantial sum of money; I sat back, took a deep breath and absorbed the events of the day: I was now 25 and it seems that there was no turning back from my status as a married woman.

We spent our first two nights at a local hotel and the following week in Cornwall: I was desperate to have a honeymoon abroad but Arif did not have a right of residence so we were stranded in the UK. The reality of marriage beyond our own relationship had still not exposed itself and so, I continued to live in my bubble full of bliss and blessings.

And the bubble was to remain intact for quite some time yet: just a week before my wedding day, I had managed to secure a job in Halifax, close to Dewsbury, but my contract did not start till the first of September. I had therefore decided to continue working at my school in Bolton till the end of the academic year. This left one whole term of limbo between our wedding day and my new job in Halifax. The only solution was for our marriage to become part time temporarily. For almost fourteen weeks we only lived with each other at weekends, making the relationship exciting and interesting as well as delaying the reality of living away from the security of my own family.

A month after our wedding day, we had yet another matrimonial ceremony: this time at the marriage registration office. Although most Muslim couples do eventually register their marriage in the UK, there is never any rush to complete the formality. However, Arif needed the marriage certificate as part of the documentation to help him achieve British citizenship. The event was yet another happy occasion. Confetti, family photos and food were all part of the celebrations. The element that was dramatically reduced was the number of guests and the personal touch that this allowed made the celebration far more intimate.

Our weekend marriage continued for another month but as the summer holidays drew closer, I realised that soon I would no longer be a guest at my in-laws but a member of the family. My life was about to change and I could only pray that I would deal with the changes in a manner that would allow me to remain true to myself whilst respecting the routines and behaviours of Arif's family.

Chapter Thirty-one

Reality bites

My bubble of bliss began to seep its delights as the reality of living with the in-laws started to sink in. I could not lay any fault on my in-laws: they were simply continuing to live as they had always done, but I found my intrusion into another family's physical space, mannerisms and attitudes difficult to conform to. From the first 'real' day of living there, I felt claustrophobic: claustrophobic in terms of where I could sit, in which position I was to sit; I had a limit to how much I could say before I was bordering on disrespectful; my voice could only be raised to a certain level before it became unruly; I was not free to dress how I pleased in the presence of my in-laws and I could not express my true emotions in case I was to offend or upset anyone.

The most challenging aspect of living with a family of strangers is the constraint it puts on one's personality. Holding back the natural instinct to jump to my own defence during moments of injustice felt like I was betraying my very identity. It was only when I was in the privacy of my bedroom that I could speak my true mind, venting out all my frustrations on the only person that allowed my true self come to life.

Thankfully, Arif truly understood my loss of emotional freedom. He was not shocked when I revealed to him that I would shed tears every other day in the bathroom, where I was guaranteed privacy, just to release some of the frustrations of having to hold back on my emotions. Arif also felt the same feelings of constraint when he moved to England. Even though he had moved in with his blood relatives, he lacked the emotional bond that develops between parents and siblings from childhood. He would also find himself crying, missing his grandparents and friends back in India as well as the lifestyle, which was a stark contrast to his life in England.

Arif's mum was told to leave him in India at the age of one and was forced to immigrate to England on her own, being told that her chances of being granted a visa would be far greater if she declared herself single and childless. Just like my mum, she was a subservient wife and daughter, so despite her meek attempts at opposing the decision, she was left with no choice. For seven years she worked in the cotton mills in Bolton, placing the brown envelope on the fireplace every week for the family that she boarded with, desperately missing her family back in India. After seven years her husband arrived in the UK and they moved to Dewsbury. They had two more children in Britain whilst fitting in regular trips to India to visit Arif.

Often they would be bearing exciting gifts and expensive clothes to compensate for the fact that he was not at home with them. It was only once Arif was eighteen that they made efforts to settle him in to the UK and it was this dramatic change in his life that Arif initially found difficult to adapt to.

After a year of marriage, and a year of suffering my own emotional turmoil through sharing a home with the in-laws, I decided to take a step back and assess my handling of the situation: there was no doubt that my tears were genuine, but how long could I continue to torture myself in this way? Arif could only listen and my in-laws could not be blamed – I realised that I was the only one who could control my emotive state through spiritual deliberation. I needed to put my trust in Allah, focusing on the positives rather than giving all my attention to my emotional needs. It was clear that as long as I was living with my in-laws I would always have to hold back on certain aspects of my personality. There were many attractive attributes to my in-laws that were scarce in other homes and it was these qualities that I concentrated on. I had forgotten how to be grateful by wasting my energy on an emotional state that was not a necessity. By training myself with this approach, I found that the flow of tears dried up and I became a happier person on the inside.

And the act of becoming grateful was rewarded with Arif officially becoming a British Citizen! As soon as he received the little red book that represented the freedom to travel we booked a sunshine week away to Turkey. The escape from reality was timed perfectly – feeling like a celebration after the personal battle with my internal thoughts had been won.

As soon as we returned from Turkey we celebrated our first year of marriage and prayed that we would experience many more years of happiness. Despite the lack of privacy, our relationship was becoming stronger. We could communicate our thoughts and feelings to each other with ease and because of our mutual calm demeanours, we were able to listen to each other without becoming impatient or irritated. I could sense the love developing between us as we shared our lives together, aspiring to similar goals and ambitions. I never blamed Arif for the fact that we were living with his family: it was something I had always expected and was dealing with in my own way. My blameless attitude towards Arif only served to increase the respect between us and I was praying that my attempt at keeping the peace with his family would also be accepted as a form of worship by God.

Once our marriage approached the two year mark, I reminded Arif of the sensitive subject of buying our own home. Because of my mother-in-law's difficult past, she suffered from bouts of serious depression and so, I was instructed by Arif not to go in guns blazing. He told me that he would handle the matter in his own way, but several weeks went by without any mention of our plans. Soon the opportunity to reveal our intentions came up in conversation and I made sure that the beans were well and truly spilt.

We were in the kitchen – my mother in law was making the curry whilst I rolled out the chapattis. We were discussing marriage and how difficult it was becoming to find a spouse through the arranged marriage process. I told her about some of my experiences then seized the opportunity to tell her about the condition that I always used to set: the one about moving out after two years. She looked at me suspiciously then asked me if that was my intention now. As I nodded my head in the affirmative she responded with silence. It wasn't what she wanted to hear. Arif had given her the impression before our marriage that he would live with his mum forever to compensate for the fact that she had missed eighteen years of his life - yet he had never voiced any opposition to the two of us living in our own home whenever we discussed the subject. It was yet another example of a lack of parent-child communication – a common occurrence in my second family - and one that usually led to misunderstanding and upset.

When I told Arif about my conversation with his mother he seemed annoyed yet relieved. I had completed the difficult task of confronting his mum on his behalf, which was a positive, yet he was annoyed with me because I had simply come out and said it! When I asked him what other strategy he had in mind to deliver news of our plans, he had no clear line of attack.

My now late father-in-law had supported our decision from the onset. He understood that we needed to move on with our lives: to own our own property, have more responsibility and become independent from the apron strings that pulled us back from becoming a family in our own right. Arif's late grandmother was also in the UK at this time and she also supported our decision. And so, with my in-laws help and advice, we began our search for the home that, if God willed, would bring us many years of contentment.

Our search for a home was combined with the attempt to start a family. Ever since my own childhood, I had always adored little children so it only seemed natural to have a few of my own. Arif however, had no desire to bring his own little mini-me in to the world. His childhood was unique: with his parents hundreds of miles away, he was bought up mollycoddled by his grandparents - protected from pain and overcompensated with love. He did not experience the joy of sharing a childhood with little siblings and countless cousins so the idea of babies and annoying toddlers did not appeal to him. Arif was also adamant that children would interfere with our relationship as well as taking away our freedom. However, from my point of view there was no question of a marriage without children, so Arif's uncommon stance on a marriage without children was dismissed by me as soon as he uttered the words!

Two months after the decision to give up the contraception I discovered that I was pregnant. Arif took the news with a pinch of salt, but I more than compensated for his nonchalance. The prospect of motherhood excited me. I had been told countless times of my natural, calming influence on children by my aunties whose young children I had frequently looked after. Motherhood felt like the obvious next step in my life and I was grateful that I had been given the opportunity to celebrate my maternal instincts.

It was around the revelation of this good news that we also secured our own property: a small, four bedroom detached house with a big garden and an en suite bathroom: the home that I had always wanted. At the time, over a decade ago, the asking price of the property of £92,000 seemed extortionate, but our joint salaries were substantial enough to qualify for a mortgage. Within weeks the house became our home – be it only during the night time. Our move was to be a gradual process so as to not shock my mother-in-law in to a state of depression. I was happy to accept these terms as I was truly appreciative of the fact that my first home resembled the home that I had pictured myself in many years in to the future - it was enough that for a small part of the day we could enjoy the luxury of privacy and free reign within our very own four walls.

Chapter Thirty-two

Introducing a new life

I had a perfect pregnancy: no morning sickness; not a hint of nausea; a beautiful round bump with no sign of unwanted fat; one lonesome stretch mark and no discomfort with heartburn or indigestion. The gentle kicks of my unborn baby felt miraculous as it developed without any complications.

Narrated by Abdullah (r.a), Allah's Messenger (peace be upon him) said:-"(As regards to your creation), every one of you is collected in the womb of his mother for the first 40 days, and then he becomes a clot for another 40 days, and then a piece of flesh for another 40 days. Then Allah (s.w.t) sends an angel to write 4 words: He writes his deeds, time of his death, means of his livelihood, and whether he will be wretched or blessed (in the Hereafter). Then the soul is breathed into his body. (Bukhari)

I knew how blessed I was to experience such an uncomplicated, comfortable pregnancy. It was only during the final few weeks that my body complained about the load that it was carrying. Cramp, exhaustion and the frustrations of not being able to move freely took over as I waited with impatient fear for the contractions to begin.

I didn't have long to wait: just one day over my due date, on the night of the 23rd of August 2002, my body gave to me the first signal that the fun was about to begin! I was in the bathroom, emptying my bladder for the second time that night, when a gush of water exited my body and landed straight in to the toilet bowl – the timing was impeccable: not a single drop of my broken waters found its way on to the bathroom floor!

I was experiencing what seemed like mild contractions, but with my waters broken, we decided to visit the hospital. After being examined, I was sent back home and told to return when my contractions were closer together.

We went directly to my mother-in-law's house, ready to wait out the contractions until the pain became intolerable. I was fed old-age remedies that claimed to speed up the labour process and given plenty of support and sympathy. After eight hours of painful pacing back and forth in my in-law's front room I reached the point where I could no longer tolerate the excruciating pain. Arif drove me to the hospital and after another examination they said that I was not dilated enough and that labour was still several hours away. Due to it being my first pregnancy, they allowed me to stay at the hospital and fitted me up with an epidural, as I had requested in my birth plan, to help with the agonizing pain.

It was now the 24th of August. The midwives continued

to poke and prod, assessing the health of the baby and determining the time of delivery. I was comfortable: the machinery that I was plugged into indicated when I was experiencing a contraction as the epidural had numbed the sensation of pain in the lower half of my body. After several hours, when I was ten centimetres dilated, the pain numbing drug was no longer allowed to enter my bloodstream: it was time to deliver my baby and if my body was topped up with more epidural, I would not experience the sensation to push, leaving me with no control over the process of pushing the baby out.

I was transferred on to the labour ward where I was allowed to find some solace from the now intolerable pain by breathing in gas and air through a hand held pipe. The drug was a heavenly substitute for the epidural. Every few minutes an excruciating contraction would invade my body: intense backache would make its ways around to my pelvis and groin area, making me scream with agony. The pain would continue to pierce through my body for a few minutes until it gradually subsided, only to begin again a few minutes later.

Arif remained by my side, wishing he had worn metal gloves as I crushed the bones of his hand every time I had a contraction. He could only watch helplessly, repeating reassurances that meant nothing at the time, praying that it would soon be over.

At this point, I had lost all dignity. I lay sprawled on the bed, constantly shifting positions, screaming with pain and not caring who was walking in and out of the room. The effects of the gas and air and the extreme pain made the experience surreal – I felt that I was trapped in a bizarre world of floating footsteps and dancing voices that had an extremely limited vocabulary consisting of just a few words push – you're nearly there, push!

I called them all liars. It was all part of a plan to keep me part of this bizarre scene. There was no baby…I just had to keep pushing…forever! Arif told me that he could see the top of the baby's head but I continued to accuse him of fabricating the whole thing! One more push they said and that would be the end. I was sapped of all energy, yet when the contraction came, my body knew what I had to do. Yet still, the push was not strong enough. I lowered my hand to feel the top of the head that had allegedly found its way out hoping to motivate myself, and sure enough, I felt a head of rough, sticky hair.

The contractions, pain and screams of agony continued for another hour. It was becoming increasingly difficult to find the motivation or energy to push as the baby's head remained lodged in my uterus. Even though its heart rate was steady, I could sense the atmosphere in the room change. The mid-wife's tone of voice became more authoritative as she asked me to push using every last drop of energy left in my body at the next contraction.

Following her orders, I gathered all the power remaining in my exhausted body and pushed for as long as I could. Thankfully, the baby managed to slide out of me, landing safely in the mid-wife's arms. She quickly wrapped it in a towel and after a few checks, placed it on my chest. Arif's eyes filled with tears, expressing a huge sense of relief as well as the joy of becoming a father.

I was overcome with joy too, but not because of the gooey baby that now lay on my chest waiting for motherly love but because the nightmare that I was trapped in, for what seemed like an eternity, was finally over. As the midwife injected my thigh to help bring on the delivery of the placenta, I lay on the bed utterly exhausted. It was only a few minutes later, when both Arif and I recovered some of our sanity, that we realized we hadn't checked the sex of the baby. We lifted up the blanket and peered in between the baby's legs. Our indifference to the sex of the baby meant that we were happy either way but Arif must have felt a small pang of delight when he saw that our first-born was a boy. We also noticed how his head was considerably large in proportion to the rest of his body, explaining why it took so long to push him out.

Just as I was beginning to enjoy our new arrival, a crowd of doctors and midwives began to gather around the foot of the bed. They were observing the aftermath of my labour: I was bleeding heavily and had torn from one end to the other. The one last push that I was asked to perform had been detrimental in causing the bleeding and the frightening tear. A gentle, controlled cut would have been far less destructive but the professional in whose hands I was entrusted had not had the insight to see this.

Rasulullah (Sallallahu alayhi wasallam) said: "*The woman that dies in her virginity or during her pregnancy or at the time of birth or thereafter (in nifaas) will attain the rank of a martyr.*"

I was to be taken in to theatre and be given twenty-two internal and external stitches in between my legs. There was no time to panic or become flustered, but before I was rolled in to the operating theatre, I insisted on being topped up with more epidural: pain was not an option!

My legs were placed in to stirrups, as I lay back, comforted by the fact that I felt nothing below the waist. As the stitching operation began, I felt the sensation of the needle making its way in and out, through my skin, but there was no pain. Three people were performing the task of sewing me back together, whilst another three professionals monitored my general health and kept me supplied with epidural. As I played my part in this strange spectacle, a spectacle that was a part of everyday life for the professionals, we discussed mundane matters such as cooking the tea and decorating the house. The moment felt like an eccentric art movie: the enactment of an out of the ordinary scene was being performed yet the characters remained immune to it, indulging in conversation that made no reference to the peculiarity around them.

For the next five days I was imprisoned within the walls of the hospital. With the exception of a couple of nurses, most of the staff on the ward displayed a cold, impersonal attitude. Even on the first night, when I had a urinary catheter attached to my body and the effect of the epidural left me paralyzed from the waist down, I was blatantly told to pick my own crying son up when I requested some assistance in taking him out of his incubator cot. The following morning, when I woke up after very little sleep, I discovered the bottom half of my bed sheet covered with my blood, and as the nurse changed the sheets, blood dripped on to the carpeted floor near my bed, yet the potential hazard of infection was ignored.

Arif spent most of the day in the hospital, trying to come to terms with the responsibility of fatherhood as well as handling the tar like poo that our son was so expertly producing every few hours. Each day we would go through the motions of bathing, feeding, changing nappies and bonding with our son, but yet each day felt like an eternity. I was desperate to leave the hospital, but my release would only come when the doctors were satisfied that I was on the road to recovery.

My stitches were uncomfortable and painful. Every movement I made required a conscious effort to avoid pain. I felt no joy in taking care of my newborn baby as the agony of the operation dominated my mind. Every urge to go to the bathroom filled me with dread. The doctors were waiting for me to successfully pass stools and prescribed plenty of lactose to ensure a comfortable ride, but this was of little solace to me. I envisioned unbearable suffering, resulting in stress, which only delayed my ticket to freedom.

After five days I was granted the freedom I yearned for, when my body finally released its much-awaited load. Thankfully, the lactose efficiently played its role, making the experience painless. The doctors gave me permission to take my son, who we named Sajid, home and as I waited for Arif to collect us, I breathed a huge sigh of relief that I was finally leaving the inhospitable hospital.

Chapter Thirty-three

The end of life as we know it

Life was never the same again. With a child now the centre of our lives, our personal needs and desires became secondary to the demands of our son. Between the nappy changing and feeding, I continued to soak my body morning and night in the bath to gradually melt the sutures that were helping my body to heal the tear. To reduce the pain of movement, I adopted the 'John Wayne walk': a side-to-side step that avoided unnecessary friction: I had a picture perfect pregnancy, but the after-effects of a difficult labour were truly testing my endurance.

Six months after the traumatic experience of childbirth my body had finally recovered from the shock, but motherhood did not come as naturally to me as I had anticipated. I often lost patience with the continuous cries of colic during the nights and the constant demands for food and fresh nappies throughout the day. The occasional moments of bonding that I did share with Sajid were not powerful enough to compensate for the frustrations of the incessant demands on my time.

Arif tried his best to make my life easier but fatherhood was not an easy transition for him either. Together, we worked through the sleepless nights and reassured each other by the fact that the unremitting cries for attention were not going to last forever. Eventually, the joy of becoming parents had to outweigh all its frustrations.

And of course, that day came. It was the day when we made the decision to try for another baby: being prepared to experience the whole journey again was an obvious indication that the worst was over. Our son was now nearly three years old, out of nappies and a daily source of pleasure in our lives. We were settled and happy in our new home. The decision to have another baby however was not borne out of emotional bliss: it was more a practical decision. I didn't want an only child in the house so the only solution was to produce a sibling for him.

I fell pregnant straight away and was soon leaving my school in Halifax for a second maternity leave. Again, I was blessed with a perfect pregnancy and because this was my second time round, I also felt more confident with the changes my body was experiencing. When the time for giving birth approached, I no longer had the fear of the unknown so I delayed going to the hospital until my contractions were only five minutes apart. My waters broke in the car and within an hour of arriving there I had given birth to a healthy baby girl. To avoid the traumatic experience of the last labour, I instructed the midwife to give me a snip of a centimetre or two just as the intensity of the labour heightened. This resulted in a mere three stitches compared to the twenty-two I had to endure the last time. After just one night I was back home, healthy and grateful that I did not have to endure the months of discomfort that I had previously experienced.

Motherhood was far more relaxed this time round. I have no doubt that it was my lack of experience and the over-reaction to every little whimper and cry that prevented me from enjoying the experience of my first born, but with our daughter, who we named Aliyah, the process was far less stressful even though she presented us with an abundance of challenges to overcome.

Once my perfectly balanced family of four had been created, time seemed to move far quicker. I was no longer measuring the years with the passing of my life, but with the constantly changing years of my children. They moved from nappies to potties and from playgroups to classrooms with incredible speed, as they became young, independent little people with ever-changing, truly entertaining personalities.

I continued to teach, moving from the school in Halifax to one in Dewsbury. My mother-in-law had looked after my children when they were babies and she continued to take care of them for the time between them leaving school and my arriving at home. After Aliyah's birth, Arif had retired from the world of being an employee and had moved into the unpredictable world of running his own business. As his office was located within our neighbourhood, it gave us the flexibility we needed in terms of school runs and days of sickness.

Life moved at a quick pace. My children accelerated in their physical and social development. After a few years of working at my school in Dewsbury, both of them were in full time education, making the week run a lot smoother. They demonstrated natural talent academically, so it was not necessary for me to tutor them outside of school hours: something I considered to be a true blessing, as I had neither the motivation nor the energy to continue teaching after I left work.

They were also attending mosque every day after school for two hours. Just as I spent most of my evenings during my childhood learning to read Arabic and memorizing prayers, so they also continued the tradition, however, there experience was far more structured than mine ever was! My children have a curriculum to follow and their teachers have some Islamic educational background to support their teaching. The mosque they attend houses upright toilet cubicles as opposed to glorified holes in the ground and there are strict rules and regulations that control the use of physical punishment in the classrooms.

There are countless other memories that I could continue to share about my children but that would require the authoring of another book! Significant events and influential people also continued to enter my life creating reminiscences that deserve a mention, but again, neither time nor print allows for such a luxury. What cannot be omitted is the change that I experienced within myself that led to a dramatic transformation in my attitude towards life, softening my heart and helping me to express deep gratitude for all the positivity in my life.

Chapter Thirty-four

The meaning of life

At the age of thirty five I was fulfilling my vision of the perfect life: a happy marriage, two beautiful children, a handful of friends who understood me, a steady social life and a modest, detached home. But I was not yet at the end of my search in finding the real me. There was still a sense of emptiness: a vacant space that was yearning to be filled by something other than the material – and despite our dedicated belief in the unseen, like so many of the people around me, I was too busy getting through each day to truly consider the purpose of my existence and to make active changes that could improve my inner self. Religion was a big part of my identity and I knew that if I delved deeper into its call to live a life of piety and charity, I would find the answers that would fill the lingering emptiness within me. However this required commitment: I was blinded by the many demands of daily life and had little trust in my ability to fulfil the obligations of a deeply dedicated follower of faith, so I resisted the road to commitment, choosing to tread the path of a moderate Muslim where God remained in the background, rather than at the forefront of my daily routines and decisions.

My lax attitude and stubborn refusal to self-reflect on the

deeper meaning of my own existence was however challenged just a few weeks before my thirty-sixth birthday in the form of a dream. It was a dream that I found impossible to ignore, as it seemed to be warning me against the consequences of continuing to live my life without any sincere effort to bring myself closer to God.

There was a river in the dream: a fast flowing river with several people struggling to keep their head above the water – including myself. This river represented hell. All those walking next to the river were dwellers of paradise. They walked along the path elated that they had reached their goal having pleased God with their many good deeds. My arms were reaching above the water, hoping that someone would help me to escape the pull of hell that was trying to drag me in. Eventually, my mother-in-law passes by and attempts to save me. Whether she did or not remains a mystery as I woke up as soon as she grabbed my arms.

Although it was just a dream, for many days afterwards the significance of what I had seen continued to dominate my consciousness. I could still feel the anguish and desperation of drowning in a world of punishment and anger, but at the same time there was the sweet smell of paradise inviting me in to a peaceful, spiritually enlightening haven. I was happy for my mother-in-law, who seemed to have settled in to paradise with ease, and, according to my dream, my attitude towards her in this world would influence my own destiny in the after-life.

Islam's foundations are built upon the belief in the hereafter, so the strong representation of heaven and hell in my dream, and the struggle that I faced between them, gave me the motivation I needed to pull myself out of the water and begin to see the light that would guide me towards the paradise that all Muslims hope to enter.

"And the life of this world is nothing but play and amusement. But far better is the house in the hereafter for those who are Al-Muttaqun (the pious). Will you not then understand?" (Quran, Al-An'aam: 32)

"Our Lord, give us in this world that which is good, and in the hereafter that which is good, and save us from the torment of the fire." (Quran, 2:201)

The change was gradual, with many moments of deep reflection and research, in the hope that the decisions I made were faithful to the demands of God and to me. Commitment was the key to my transformation: without a heartfelt decision full of love and hope for my faith, I could easily falter in my quest to fill my heart with God.

So where was I to begin? Was I to change my outward appearance, in the hope that the physical reminder of who I was would encourage the inner me to change? Or should I commit to hours of meditation, praying that God would come to me, pleased with my endless supplication? The answers to my pursuit for spirituality were not clear but God had provided me with the starting point and I knew that it was now my decision to either choose the path towards change or to dismiss my dream and continue travelling on the road of spiritual moderation where my relationship with God would remain sedentary.

My conscience made the decision for me: a lack of spirituality in my day-to-day existence distanced me from my faith that led to my thoughts being dominated by personal needs and desires. To enable me to truly display a sense of gratitude I needed to make room in my heart for God that in turn, God willing would motivate me to make a difference to the lives of others.

The opportunity to take the first step towards change came just a few weeks after the dream: I was going out for a meal with some friends who all happened to wear headscarves. As yet, I had not adhered to this part of the Islamic dress code and despite a part of my conscience resisting the change; I fought with it and decided that this was a chance for me to progress with my mission to a stronger faith.

The Quran states:

"Say to the believing man that they should lower their gaze and guard their modesty; that will make for greater purity for them; and Allah is well acquainted with all that they do. And say to the believing women that they should lower their gaze and guard their modesty; and that they should not display their beauty and ornaments except what must ordinarily appear thereof; that they should draw their veils over their bosoms and not display their beauty except to their husbands, their fathers, their husbands' fathers, their sons, their husbands' sons, their brothers or their brothers' sons, or their sisters' sons, or their women, or the slaves whom their right hands possess, - (Qur'an 24:30-31)

There are many interpretations of the dress code for Muslim women and often Muslim women in the Western world will make independent choices as to how they present themselves to society. I had considered my style of dress modest from the Western point of view but hidden away at the back of my mind I always knew that God would not be happy with my negligence of His words. Attention and compliments from others boosted my self-esteem encouraging me to preen myself to the non-Muslim concept of beauty. Yet Islam has its own concept of how beauty should be displayed. There is great emphasis on protecting the woman from the unlawful gaze of lustful men: as Rasulullah (Sallallahu Alaihi Wa Sallam) is reported to have said, *"May the curse of Allah be on the one who looks lustfully and on the one who is looked at with lust."*

The dress code exists to grant liberation for women through a form of dress that states without any ambiguity that she is a Muslim woman who does not require the attention of others to feel attractive. Islam asks of the sincerely faithful to be satisfied with their love for Allah and not desire the admiration or flattery of others to fulfil the needs of the heart. It is a deeply challenging concept: to forego all forms of flattery and be truly satisfied and at peace with one's love for God, yet once achieved, it is an incredible freedom that releases one from the stronghold of social expectations and conditioning.

I had a long journey ahead of me before I was to reach the pinnacle of inner peace, but wearing the headscarf was a positive start. Although I accepted that covering my hair was a part of my faith, for most of my life it was something that I never considered doing. Weakness in faith justified my reasons through excuses such as feeling self-conscious about the reaction from others, a fear of being non-committal and the claustrophobic manner in which it is worn, restricting freedom of movement.

But now the headscarf became a part of my identity and wearing it outside the home boosted my own confidence about my faith. There was an unspoken respect from my Muslim brothers that I hadn't experienced before and it served as a constant physical reminder that I followed a faith that required the daily remembrance of God: my sincere intentions in the action had enabled me to get closer to God and this favour that He had bestowed upon me encouraged me to search for further means by which God would open up my heart to Him.

The next and most powerful change came when a neighbour invited me to attend a religious gathering that was taking place at her house. I rarely committed myself to such preaching sessions and was cynical of their motives, but I agreed to attend for the sake of our friendship. The ladies in the gathering consisted of the local residents, who took it in turns to read from a book of Hadiths, like those included in this autobiography, and then one member of the community spent fifteen minutes discussing specific aspects of the faith. The atmosphere was informal and had an aura of peaceful, shared meditation. There were no formally trained members of the religious community, just members of the locality attempting to share their faith in the hope that God would make their hearts stronger.

When the gathering had ended, they asked for volunteers to read and discuss Islam in future meetings. My mouth remained firmly shut, as I knew that my lack of knowledge about our faith meant that I was not the ideal candidate for the job. However, my neighbour was quick off the mark and pointed out to the ladies that my teaching background would give me the confidence to speak in front of an audience. I shook my head in disagreement, protesting that I had little confidence when it came to making speeches about religion, but my protestations were in vain. The gathering was in desperate need of volunteers and a forced election of a candidate was a candidate nevertheless, so I calmed my protests and accepted the role of speaker.

Two weeks later I found myself sitting on the floor of another neighbour's house with approximately thirty women staring at me waiting for some inspiration. I had researched my speech well and spent several hours preparing the notes, determined to make my words authentic and true to Islam. The only guidance we were given came in the form of six headings: faith; prayers; knowledge and remembrance; treatment of other Muslims; sincerity of intention and the duty to spread the message of Islam. The women listened attentively as I related the six headings that summarized being a Muslim to my own life, trying to make my words reach the hearts of the audience.

As I was reeling off my well-rehearsed speech, I realized that much of what I preached, I did not practice: my performance of the five daily prayers was erratic and without the presence of heart that is expected. I was civil to others but did not go out of my way to show kindness. Sincerity was present, but I did not spend much time reflecting on its strength. As this experience had proved, my knowledge of Islam was scarce and I spent little of my time remembering God. The only step I had taken was the decision to make my faith stronger but as yet, I could not claim to have taken bona fide action that led to change.

After reflecting on my lack of action and the moments of hypocrisy during my speech at the gathering, I realized with complete devotion that the expression of my faith had to be realized through my own actions.

The Prophet said: *"Whoever has (the following) four characteristics will be a pure hypocrite: "If he speaks, he tells a lie; if he gives a promise, he breaks it, if he makes a covenant he proves treacherous; and if he quarrels, he behaves in a very imprudent evil insulting manner (unjust). And whoever has one of these characteristics has one characteristic of a hypocrite, unless he gives it up"*.

I was confident with my belief in the first pillar in Islam: to believe in God and the prophet Muhammad (peace be upon him) but my practice of the second pillar, the five daily prayers, was erratic so achieving consistency in this form of worship was my next goal. The five daily prayers are an obligatory aspect of Islam. They serve to remind the worshipper their purpose in life: to love Allah and spend as much time as possible in His remembrance.

And with that objective in mind, I began to strive for regular remembrance through the daily prayers. Progress was slow but fruitful: my intention to make my supplication sincere was rewarded with a deep spirituality and a yearning to further my relationship with God. It is at these times of prayer when a Muslim is considered to be closest to God. The worshipper is blessed by His presence and He answers to specific supplications with 'My servant has praised me' and 'this is between Me and My servant and My servant shall have what he requested.'

As my opportunities to self-reflect opened up with the increasing number of daily prayers, so I began my quest to become more active both in increasing my knowledge and understanding of Islam and to live my life according to the example set by the Prophet Muhammad (peace be upon him). Humility, modesty, respecting others and sacrificing my time to help those in need of human contact were my targets, but as a mere human being, these objectives were not going to be fulfilled to their optimum within my life time: the journey needed to be an ongoing commitment where, with every trial and tribulation in my life, I would refer to the characteristics of the Prophet Muhammad (peace be upon him) to guide me towards the right path both in my attitude towards others and my motivation when making daily decisions.

I began attending our local religious gathering regularly.

With help from a friend, a weekly study class was held at my house run by a qualified Islamic teacher. At the class, we learnt to recite Arabic correctly, making the sound of each letter in the Quran resonate with the purity of its meaning. This authenticity in recitation enabled my heart to feel the words of the Quran and developed a genuine love in reading the holy book that I had rarely experienced before.

And just as my commitment to my faith was gathering momentum so God intervened by releasing more of my worldly time. Arif's business had achieved a moderate level of success and we were blessed with sufficient income to allow me to stop working. At the age of thirty-seven and after sixteen years of being committed to a career in teaching I could happily walk away from the profession, confident that my life would continue to be filled with meaningful actions.

With more time on my hands, I began to attend Arabic classes, giving myself the opportunity to translate the words of Allah. With countless on-line Islamic courses available free on the Internet, I seized the opportunity to listen to learned scholars, who discussed matters of the heart from an Islamic point of view. The more knowledge I gained, the more I fell in love with my faith. Every word I read or heard encouraged a life of peace: a plea to trust in God alone and to deal with both life's troubles and joys through His purpose.

I stepped out of my comfort zone by volunteering weekly at a care home for the disabled, challenging my personal attitudes and stereotypes about those who have to live with the after effects of strokes as well as life-time disabilities such as cerebral palsy and multiple sclerosis. Although the initial visit was upsetting, within weeks I became part of the community and developed relationships with the residents that were both heart-warming and rewarding.

As the words that I preached in the initial community gathering became a part of my everyday reality so the overwhelming love of Allah increased in my heart. With each day, the obstacles that hindered my journey towards a deeper faith were being removed: I felt that God was running towards me, embracing my heartfelt desire to encapsulate all His blessings in every moment of my life. Divine intervention had entered my heart and the tears that rolled down my face with every prayer I made in the presence of God confirmed that my emotional state could not be explained through earthly reasoning – it was His divine presence that was leaving me trembling with utter humility and praise.

Anas reported from the Prophet, may Allah bless him and grant him peace, in what he reported from his Lord, the Mighty and Majestic. He said, *"When the slave comes towards Me a hand-span, I go an arm-length towards him. When he comes towards Me an arm-length, I go a fathom towards him. When he comes towards Me walking, I go towards him running."* [al-Bukhari]

A simple flick of a hot water switch can now reduce me to tears as I feel a deep appreciation for the blessings of instant hot water. Every mouthful of food that I consume has become a favour from Allah and I no longer take for granted my ability to effectively use all my limbs and senses.

Abu Hurayra said that the Messenger of Allah, may Allah bless him and grant him peace, said, *" When I love him, I become his hearing with which he hears, his seeing with which he sees, his hand with which he strikes, and his foot with which he walks. If he were to ask Me for something, I would give it to him. If he were to ask Me for refuge, I would give him refuge.'"* [al-Bukhari]

It was at this point in my life that I felt truly fulfilled: I had been blessed with the Divine light that was to guide me for the rest of my life and I have a sincere determination to remain loyal to the favour that Allah has bestowed upon me. Every day I pray He will continue to bless me with the joy of a faith that exudes peace, love and acceptance.

Chapter Thirty-five

The heart of Islam

My penultimate chapter is about the spiritual journey that I made to Mecca in October of 2012. God's call to visit the heart of Islam came at the perfect time: my heart, mind, body and soul were all ready for the experience of my life and I was confident that the pilgrimage would continue to strengthen my faith.

The Kabah that is at the centre of Masjid Al-Haram in Mecca is the direction where Allah ordained all believers to turn to, whilst in prayer. It is directly below His throne in the heavens where His angels are in constant circumambulation. Because of its history and the many times it is mentioned in the Quran, the place of the Kabah is considered the most holy Islamic place on Earth. The small, cubed building may not rival other famous buildings; however, it is its historical significance and its close relation to God Himself that gives it the power to draw all Muslims towards it. Its impact on the human race, to this day, remains unmatched and it was this powerful pull that was drawing me in.

Every act of Hajj reminds Muslims of the noble family of Ibrahim (AS) since every act of Hajj refers back to the righteous actions and struggle of either Ibrahim (AS), his wife Hajrah or his son Ismail (AS). The history of this family teaches spiritual lessons of complete devotion to Allah and sincerity to Him. It holds an enlightening message for everybody, a father, a mother, a son and a wife.

And this was the journey that I was blessed to take, together with my husband and my sister and brother-in-law. Although we weren't altogether for our stay in the hotels, we shared the experience of the actual pilgrimage together: the five days devoted wholly to the re-enactment of the struggles of Ibrahim AS and his family. Once in Mecca, it is obligatory to visit the mosque and the Kabah as soon as possible, performing rituals that represent the actions of Ibrahim AS, his wife Hajrah and his son Ismail AS. Whilst there, I wrote a diary, and this is how I interpreted my experience of seeing the Kabah – 'the black cube' – for the first time in my life:

This is the most exciting thing I have ever done in my life. It's surreal. After a short nap, I am sitting in my hotel room full of anticipation about seeing the Kabah for the first time. I fear disappointment – an anti-climax, like so many moments in life where the reality doesn't quite match the hype, but that fear diminishes as I recall the words uttered by those who have already experienced this, the words that tell of how there are no words to describe what I was about to experience....

...I'm back. I was an emotional wreck. We walked into the mosque where the Kabah takes central place, head down. I was sobbing with every step that I took closer to the heart of who I was. Then, as we found the perfect spot to take it all in, Arif told me to look up. I was spiritually overwhelmed. My body shook with the Kabah's overpowering sense of peace and dominance. This black cube, which was so much bigger in proportion than the ground it stood on, compared to the images I had seen on the television, had an aura of tranquillity. The shared spirit and oneness to Allah shook my very existence. Tears rolled down uncontrollably as I asked Allah to grant all my prayers as He saw fit. Then I prayed wholeheartedly for my dad, who has pancreatic cancer, to remain healthy and happy and be ready to accept the time when Allah wishes him to return to Him. Tears of repentance, tears of joy and tears of utter gratefulness for the invitation to visit Allah's blessed house flowed from my tired eyes as I continued to convince myself that I was still standing in the real world and not in a state of transition to the next: it was this feeling that is impossible to express with just words – a feeling that your soul is moving away from the present and in to an unknown world where there is nothing but peace and love.

After several minutes of pure spirituality and personal pleas to the only One who truly listens, we began our circumambulation of the Kabah. As we walked slowly amongst the crowds of like-minded pilgrims I pondered over the fact that seventy-thousand angels were performing the exact form of worship in the heavens directly above us – what a privilege it was to be chosen by Allah to be in His presence worshipping him in the same manner as His angels.

More tears flowed as I continued to appeal to Allah for His mercy, to sincerely supplicate my gratitude for the many privileges in my life compared to others and to pray for the well being of my family and friends. I begged for a peaceful afterlife and a worldly existence where I would put Allah at the forefront of every decision that I made.

After the seven-round circumambulation, we were lucky enough to find a clear spot close to the Kabah to pray our two-rakah salah – thanking and praising Allah for the building of the Kabah through the prophet Ibrahim AS. At home, I would prostate many times in a day and imagine this moment to help me to feel the spirituality of the prayer, yet now, as I bowed down to prostrate there was no need for fantasy – the Kabah was just a few metres away from me. Again, uncontrollable tears rolled down my face and my whole body shook with the reality of the moment. How could anything ever beat this?

It was a moment that took my soul to another world. Next, we walked over to the zam zam (holy water) taps and as we drank the water facing the Kabah we asked Allah to keep us healthy through the blessings of His water.

To complete our Umrah (obligatory re-enactments) we were to perform the Sa'ee: a walk from the small mount of Al-Safaa to the mount of Al-Marwah. This was a re-enactment of Hajrah's experience (may Allah be pleased with her), who was the mother of Ismail RA and the wife of Ibrahim AS. She was left alone at the side of the Kabah with her son. Ibrahim AS walked away from his family by order of Allah, leaving them with some dates and a little water. His wife Hajrah trusted her husband and was aware that he was following the orders of Allah. When Ibrahim AS was a short distance away he supplicated to Allah to take care of his family and give them the strength to pass the test that they were about to receive from Allah.

Once the water and dates ran out, Hajira walked to the nearest mountain of Al Safa to look out for any possible signs of help. Having no luck and by now, being distressed, she made her way hastily to the mount of Al Marwah, but again no luck. Between the trek from one mountain to the other, Hajrah came across certain areas where her young son Ismail AS was out of sight. At this point, she would run in haste until her son was back in view. This distance is shown by green lights at the mosque and the men are expected to run at this point in honour of Hajrah's devotion to her son. Hajrah crossed the mounts back and forth seven times until she finally fell to her knees and supplicated to

Allah. Soon she heard the voice of Allah's angel. After calming herself she made her way back to her son. Near the Kabah, where Ismail lay, she saw water flowing – a reward of sustenance from Allah for her patience and faith. Hajrah rushed towards the water and shouted 'zam zam' which means 'stop stop' to control the gushing water in to a steady flow and the flow hasn't stopped since.

This act of running between the hills of Safa and Marwa by a woman was so much loved by Allah that Allah has made running between Safa and Marwa compulsory for every man and woman who performs Hajj. Allah mentions in the Quran:

"Behold! Safa and Marwa are among the Symbols of Allah"
[Surah Baqara:158]

Once we had completed our Saee (trek between Safa and Marwa), our Umrah was completed. This was something every pilgrim had to do when they first entered Mecca. To symbolise the completion of the Umrah and to symbolise the shedding away of sins Arif had his hair cut short and I trimmed an inch from my hair. Then we could leave the state of 'Ihram', where the use of scents, purposely rubbing the skin so that hair falls out and the clipping of nails are not allowed. The men also have to wear only two sheets of white cloth. There are several other acts that are not allowed whilst in the state of Ihram – acts that the Prophet Muhammad (peace be upon him) restricted himself from and are still applicable today. They are there to remind us of our status as equals, a call to revert back to being human in its purest form and a taste of judgement day, where all of mankind will gather in one place.

We now had a couple of days to rest before the days of Hajj began. My sister Moneeba was already in Mecca and was keenly waiting for our arrival so that she could spend the days prior to Hajj in our hotel, which was a stone's throw from the Kabah instead of her hotel, which was an hour's walk away – she had shifted to a different hotel as the prices became extortionate when the days of Hajj got closer.

It wasn't long before Moneeba, her husband Mohsin, Arif and I again declared the intention to be in a state of Ihram. The men wrapped themselves in the two pieces of white cloth and we all went to the mosque and prayed two rakah's of salah, supplicating to Allah that we have intended to make the pilgrimage and that we are seeking His help to make our journey safe and fulfilling. A little time after sunrise the pilgrims in our group, who were intending to follow the prophet's way and walk from Mecca to Mina, gathered at our hotel. Mina was the place where Ibrahim AS and his son Ismail RA travelled through to get to the place where Ismail RA was to be sacrificed (Arafat) and also where Ibrahim AS heard whisperings of the devil to deter him from making the sacrifice that Allah had asked of him in his dreams.

Once our small group of around fifteen people, who had chosen to walk the two and a half hour journey in the blazing heat to Mina had gathered, we began to follow the mass of people all walking in the same direction. The mood was one of adrenalin paired with some anticipation. The site was inspiring – here I was, one of hundreds of thousands of pilgrims, all making their way towards one place – all driven by our desire to please Allah – and all our tongues moist with the Arabic words saying 'Oh Allah, I am present'. I felt like a true, devoted Muslim, one of millions who's only purpose at this moment in time was to fulfil our obligations towards Allah – to re-enact the journey of our beloved prophets and to truly understand the spiritual nature of becoming a soul immersed completely by our love for Him.

We continued to say the prayer of 'I am present, Oh Allah I am present. There are no partners to Allah, I am present. Praises upon Him, the bringer of goodness, the King; there is no Allah but Him:' A universal prayer chanted throughout the journey and a response to the invitation that we were so privileged to receive from Allah. As we walked through the never ending mountainous tunnels designed to ease the journey, the prayer echoed against the walls and I filled up with a true sense of what I was – a servant to Allah: I had been blessed by Him to fulfil the re-enactment of a journey that has been the highest form of worship since Islam began. This walk was not only full of spirituality, it was unique in itself…where else was I to walk side by side with millions of other followers of Islam from all over the world chanting a single prayer that filled up the air and made my hair stand on end? We were all equal – our dress, our state of purity, our intentions to Allah – we had all given up our lives back home to share a once in a lifetime experience with each other.

After several bottles of water and a few complaints of backache we finally reached our tent in Mina. My expectations of the accommodation were of well laid out mattresses in a large tent with full air conditioning and plenty of room to pray comfortably. As the sweat dripped down our bodies from the forty degrees sweltering heat, we entered into our tent only to find that my expectations were far from the reality that greeted me. The temperature seemed to increase as the thirty-five bodies that were packed tightly in to the tent created more humidity. There was only a half metre strip of carpet exposed down the middle of the tent for manoeuvrability and the air conditioning had stopped working – a huge blow to our expectations of ending our exhausting journey with the reward of a cool, comfortable room. As we lay down on our narrow sofa beds the sweat continued to drip mercilessly down our bodies. We could do nothing to help ease the extreme tiredness, and the overpowering, suppressive heat only added to our frustration. We were told that someone had been working on the air conditioning fault since the morning and after several hours, no solution had been found – it was the responsibility of the Saudi authorities to sort the problem out so our group leaders continued to make excuses as we continued to stifle in the heat.

This was our first real test. Were we to maintain our patience and focus on the reason we were there or would the problem of the heat dominate our minds? For a couple of hours I justified my frustrations by the fact that the air conditioning was part of the deal, and if I wasn't expecting it then I wouldn't be complaining, but I soon realised that I was wasting my time and energy on something that was irrelevant compared to my reasons for being there. After some meditation, I took the conscious decision to put the heat out of my mind and focus on the spirituality of the situation by engaging in prayer. During the time of the prophet, there was no air conditioning: he had no shelter or food and water on hand. I was lucky: there were cool boxes constantly being topped up with water and drinks and a kitchen adjacent to our tent providing buffets throughout the day.

After our lunch, we found the energy to visit the communal lavatories – fifteen lavatories, hole in the ground style, shared by approximately five hundred women! We had heard many horror stories about the toilets in Mina and we were about to discover if the reality matched the claims.

Ten metres before we reached the communal lavatories the whiff of urine in the air confirmed our low expectations. The concrete built nest of back-to-back toilets with an ablution area on each side consisted of ceramic holes in the ground, without the power of a flush. They each had a short piece of hose pipe attached to a tap which we could use to wash ourselves with, but the lack of a flushing system meant that the strong stench of people's remains hung in the air and we quickly adapted by learning to hold our breath when in close vicinity to them.

At first, our Britishness proved to be a hindrance during our toilet and ablution sessions. Queuing is very much a Western tradition and the Chechnyans, Turkish and many other nationalities who were classed as Europeans did not hold any value to this tradition. However, the Indian blood inside us gave us the ability to adapt quickly, and to ensure that we got into the toilet cubicles within an acceptable period of waiting time, we would hold our arms out wide in front of the cubicle which was rightfully ours to enter next and use our well practiced authoritative teacher stares to put off any potential queue jumpers.

During ablution, up to thirty women could be fighting for a space to use the five available taps. If we waited politely our turn would never come and so, we would gently muscle our way through, careful not to upset anyone yet aware that without a little assertiveness we would never make our way to the water.

In the evening we discovered the much cooler air and soft breeze outside the tents and so, we spent most of it praying outside and sitting with our husbands engaged in religious conversation and banter. There was something truly magical and inexplicable about that first evening in Mina. I felt a part of a world community: different nationalities with social conditions that ranged from the most poverty stricken to the extremely wealthy, the young to the very old and the most spiritually absorbed to the newly enlightened, all sharing a single purpose: to re-enact the actions of the prophet, hence fulfilling a commandment of Allah. There was no doubt here – no one was suggesting that religion was a fools game, a man made form of control. What I was feeling in my heart was not the consequence of the Western concept of organised religion. My soul was uplifted – a confirmation of the peace I felt at home when I succumbed to the will of God. This wasn't something my brain could analyse or put into compartments, it was simply there. I prayed that this unconditional attachment to my faith that was ever increasing in my heart would remain pure to help me live my life with Allah at the forefront of my mind in this temporary world and prepare me for the permanent world to come.

The next morning at sunrise we began the second day of our hajj experience. We were to be transported by bus to Arafat – the stretch of desert where the prophet (peace be upon him) gave his last sermon – a moving and very contemporary speech (see below) and also the place where Adam(AS) and Bibi Hawa (Eve) were re-united after they were extradited from paradise on to Earth. This piece of desert land is known as our parent's home and has much historical significance. The prophet (peace be upon him) prayed in Arafat from high noon to sunset, facing the Kabah pleading with Allah to fulfil the rights of all Muslims to come and to help us have strong, unwavering faith. Arafat is also the place where all humankind will be gathered on judgement day – it's boundaries limitless and, depending on their relationship with their faith, they will be exposed to suffering or to serenity and peace.

After praising, and thanking God, the Prophet, may God send His praises upon him said:

"O People, lend me an attentive ear, for I know not whether

after this year, I shall ever be amongst you again. Therefore, listen to what I am saying to you very carefully and take these words to those who could not be present here today.

People, just as you regard this month, this day, this city as Sacred, so regard the life and property of every Muslim as a sacred trust. Return the goods entrusted to you to their rightful owners. Hurt no one so that no one may hurt you. Remember that you will indeed meet your Lord, and that He will indeed reckon your deeds. God has forbidden you to take usury (interest); therefore all interest obligation shall henceforth be waived. Your capital, however, is yours to keep. You will neither inflict nor suffer any inequity. God has Judged that there shall be no interest and that all the interest due to Abbas ibn Abd'al Muttalib shall henceforth be waived...

Beware of Satan, for the safety of your religion. He has lost all hope that he will ever be able to lead you astray in big things, so beware of following him in small things.

People, it is true that you have certain rights with regard to your women, but they also have rights over you. Remember that you have taken them as your wives only under a trust from God and with His permission. If they abide by your right then to them belongs the right to be fed and clothed in kindness. Do treat your women well and be kind to them for they are your partners and committed helpers. And it is your right that they do not make friends with any one of whom you do not approve, as well as never to be unchaste.

297

People, listen to me in earnest, worship God, perform your five daily prayers, fast during the month of Ramadan, and offer Zakat. Perform Hajj if you have the means.

All mankind is from Adam and Eve. An Arab has no superiority over a non-Arab, nor does a non-Arab have any superiority over an Arab; white has no superiority over black, nor does a black have any superiority over white; [none have superiority over another] except by piety and good action. Learn that every Muslim is a brother to every Muslim and that the Muslims constitute one brotherhood. Nothing shall be legitimate to a Muslim which belongs to a fellow Muslim unless it was given freely and willingly. Do not, therefore, do injustice to yourselves.

Remember, one day you will appear before God and answer for your deeds. So beware, do not stray from the path of righteousness after I am gone.

People, no prophet or apostle will come after me, and no new faith will be born. Reason well, therefore, O people, and understand words which I convey to you. I leave behind me two things, the Quran and my example, the Sunnah, and if you follow these you will never go astray.

All those who listen to me shall pass on my words to others and those to others again; and it may be that the last ones understand my words better than those who listen to me directly. Be my witness, O God, that I have conveyed your message to your people."

Then, at the summit of Arafat, the revelation came down:

"…This day have I perfected your religion for you, completed My Grace upon you, and have chosen Islam for you as your religion…" (Quran 5:3)

The plains of Arafat, until recent history, were exactly that: rough desert land without shade or shelter, but as the numbers of pilgrims have increased so the need to provide shelter, food and drink has become a necessity: my expectations of a barren land, just as history had dictated, were replaced by simple tents and constructed pathways. The toilets were just as unseemly as Mina, but by now we had become accustomed to them. We were already expecting tents without air conditioning and after the practice run at Mina, it seemed that Allah had helped us to acclimatise immediately to the stifling heat. Fresh fruit and drinks were constantly provided as we caught up with our sleep ready to engage in prayers later.

After 12.00pm we made our way outside. Other pilgrims also stood, both arms raised high, facing the direction of the Kabah. Fellow pilgrims cried out loud, tears streaming, and as I did the same, I begged Allah to have mercy on me. I prayed wholeheartedly for my children's well-being, for my family and friends and most importantly, I thanked Allah for inviting me to do exactly what the prophet had done many centuries ago – to pray for the goodness of all of mankind and to express my love for Him alone.

Just after sunset, we were to leave the plains of Arafat for the open plains of Muzdaliffah. All the pilgrims left their tents to watch the sunset and pray intently; making the most of the last few minutes left before leaving the blessed land that held so many religious significances and offered a guarantee of prayers being accepted by Allah.

As darkness approached, we were herded like cattle in to gaited spaces – released only when the bus arrived to take us to Muzdaliffah. Our group consisted of up to 200 people – 200 out of two and a half million people who were all heading towards the same place. Muzdaliffah was a further step away from the luxuries of modern life. We were to spend the night under the stars, using sleeping bags laid over an uncomfortable, rocky surface. This was where the prophets (peace be upon them) had stopped over at night on their way back to Mina, and as we were re-enacting their journey: spending the night here was the next stage of our pilgrimage.

The men were still covered in their cloths of white. It

was a truly back to basics experience. Allah wanted us to return to our state of innocence – the days of early childhood where food, drink, sleep and emptying the belly were our only concerns. I no longer thought about my family back home: I didn't miss my children or longed for my bed. The physical challenges we faced only made us stronger as we discovered what really mattered in life – that if one's relationship with Allah is strong then one could survive anything whilst remaining truly humble and grateful.

Once in Muzdaliffah, outstretched boundaries of land classified into numbers to enable the Saudi authorities to maintain some control and organisation over its two and a half million annual visitors, lay in the distance in front of us. Our early arrival enabled us to be selective about where we were to settle for the night. Once set up we took in the awe-inspiring surroundings. Pilgrims continued to roll in throughout the night and the sense of all of us being God's children under His night sky overtook me. Again, we were all gathered in one place to celebrate our faith in unity and to express our desire to please Allah.

Throughout the night the empty spaces began to fill up. Just like in the mosque in Mecca, where finding a space for prayer can be difficult, so it seemed that the late arrivals were going to struggle to find a place to rest. Sleep was never going to be possible on this night, and every time we sat up there was a new line of pilgrims searching for a spot to sleep.

Inevitably, when humans come together, we get a mixture of calm, polite people together with the ill-mannered, aggressive variety. The necessity for patience was essential and ours was tried and tested several times, but a deep breath and a reminder of why we were there ensured that our spirituality and desire to please Allah remained intact.

Whilst in Muzdaliffah, despite my efforts to keep my bladder empty, I had to visit the very public toilets. I had grown accustomed to sharing the toilets with hundreds, but now the number had increased to the thousands! I reluctantly dodged my way through the numerous sprawled out pilgrims to the first block of female toilets. Whilst trying my best to hold my breath, I stood firmly in the queue. It was my turn to enter the cubicle next, and just so that there was no confusion about that fact, I stretched my arm out and placed my hand on the cubicle door, ready to enter as soon as the current occupier had exited.

As the last occupant left I began to enter, but the lady behind me attempted to physically drag me out! I had an abundance of patience but this was downright rude! Unable to accept the injustice nature of the situation I pronounced a firm, universal 'no!' The lady, who looked to be Turkish, continued to maul me, but as my voice grew louder and more dominating she backed off. Pleased with my international victory against the uncivilised world I entered the reeking cubicle as if I had entered a place of privilege...my head held high with a real sense of achievement. Ironically, there was no water, leaving me no means to wash myself, so I was out as soon as I had entered, allowing the unruly Turkish lady to enter much quicker than she deserved!

My bladder still being full, I moved on to the next set of cubicles. My stomach turned as out of the corner of my eye I spotted the sights and inevitably, the smells inside. Without water, the toilets, which were already without a flushing system, were now collecting even more horrendous materials. I decided it was time to give up and hold it in till we were back at Mina.

After collecting our stones to throw at 'Satan' or the walls that represented the whisperings of Satan, we prayed, made conversation and grabbed a few minutes of unsettled sleep in-between. Pilgrims continued to squeeze into the remaining patches of ground throughout the night to fulfil the requirement of spending part of the night within the boundaries of Muzdaliffah before sunrise.

The night passed quickly: just sitting up and taking in the mass of people was enough to keep us occupied. It is impossible to describe in words the uniqueness of spending a night under the stars with millions of other like for like spiritual souls: I will never spend another night like it unless Allah blesses me with a second journey to His blessed lands.

As sunrise approached we made ablution with the bottled water provided by the group, as the taps were far too congested. Once our prayers were said, we were to make our way back to Mina by foot as the group leader had warned us in advance that transport would not be provided after this point of the pilgrimage. After a few hours of rest in Mina, we were to walk to the place of the whisperings of Satan heard by Ibrahim AS. The pelting of the wall represents Ibrahim AS's fight against the whisperings of Satan, tempting him to forego the sacrifice of his son Ismail RA.

Without transport, we were asked to walk back to Mina with the group following one of the leaders. It was very easy to get lost amongst the thousands of identical white tents despite the street numbers. Without a good night sleep for two consecutive nights, the journey from Muzdaliffah was difficult and the sun was beginning to demonstrate its power. However, rather than focusing on the negatives, we considered the significance of making the same journey that our Muslim ancestors took and made prayers of gratitude that we too were blessed with the same experience.

As soon as we arrived back at Mina at around eight o' clock we collapsed onto our narrow but comfortable sofa beds. Mina was now luxurious accommodation compared to Arafat and Muzdaliffah: we were even fortunate enough to find that the air conditioning was now in full working order. Within minutes I was fast asleep. The group leader informed us that we were to be ready to pelt the Satan wall at 11 am so I was looking forward to the luxury of a few hours sleep. Unfortunately, just an hour later I was woken up from my deep slumber – the walk to the 'jamarat' – the bridge where Satan's wall was situated – was re-scheduled for those who wished to go early. My husband and brother in law had decided we were to be part of this early bird group. Reluctantly, and not without some complaining, I picked up the bag of stones we had collected from Muzdaliffah and dragged myself out of the tent. My semi-conscious state began the next journey – another hour's walk in the now extremely hot, baking sun. The physical hardships were now beginning to take their toll, but I knew how important it was to override the temptation to wallow in self-pity and to find the strength to absorb myself in the spirituality of the pilgrimage.

After a short struggle with my conscience I managed to win the fight. Ibrahim AS had to overcome the whisperings of Satan three times as he passed this area of Mina. He threw stones towards the voices that were tempting him to walk away from the will of Allah, however, Ibrahim AS managed to ward off the whisperings and continue with the difficult task of sacrificing his own flesh and blood for the sake of his love towards his Creator.

The Saudi authorities have constructed large, well planned-out infrastructure to help manage the millions of pilgrims that pass across the three places of the whisperings of Satan. The signs led us directly to these walls. On this occasion we only had to pelt the larger wall. We pelted the wall with seven of the forty-nine stones we collected at Muzdaliffah. At each passionate throw, we shouted 'Allah is great' then made a prayer asking Allah to protect us all from the never-ending whisperings of Satan.

As soon as we had left the bridge, Arif made the call telling the slaughterhouse that we had completed the pelting of the Satan and that our sacrifice, which would involve up to seven people paying for one animal, could go ahead. The slaughterhouses began their mammoth task of performing thousands upon thousands of sacrifices in the name of millions of pilgrims. The tonnes of meat that would be killed would be distributed throughout the world by being packed up in to tins and flown out as well as the some of the meat being eaten fresh by the pilgrims and the locals.

The sights on the way back to our hotel were unique:

along the sides of the roads were makeshift barbershops. Men who had performed the pelting and had been informed of the completion of their sacrifice were having their hair removed – a symbolic act which represented the notion of a new start: a shedding of old sins, just like a new-born baby. There was a sense of celebration and achievement as this was the moment when Ismail AS, who was just as willing to sacrifice himself for the sake of pleasing Allah, was saved. As he lay prostrated on the ground, ready for his father to lower the sword, he was replaced by a ram as Allah was satisfied that they had fulfilled the vision that He had sent them. Their commitment to their faith had been proven and an example to the followers to come had been established. There was a sense of being accepted by Allah, and hardships, although incomparable to the trials of Ibrahim AS and Ismail AS, had been overcome.

The three most difficult days of Hajj were now over. By the time we got back to our hotel the phone call had been received telling us that our sacrifice had been completed. Arif joined the long queue at the barbers next door to our hotel – ready to pay the quadrupled price for having his head shaved. It was to be the busiest day of the year for the profession and they were taking full advantage of it. I snipped an inch off my hair and dived in to the much anticipated shower.

After a long rest, we made our way to the mosque to complete the final ritual that would seal our pilgrimage. First we completed the circumambulation of the Kabah, then re-enacted Bibi Hajra's efforts of searching for water from the mounts of Al-Safah to Al-Marwah. After thanking Allah with true sincerity for making our Hajj easy and for making it a spiritually moving experience we prayed that our Hajj would be accepted and that all of humanity would benefit from Allah's invitation to worship in the blessed lands.

Although our Hajj was now officially complete, there were still acts of worship that we chose to perform as this was how the Prophet (peace be upon him) continued with his pilgrimage. Most pilgrims make their way back to Mina before sunrise of the same day that the sacrifice is performed, spending the night at Mina, pelting the Satan the following day, spending one more final night in Mina and then performing a final pelting of the Satan before heading for Mecca.

With renewed energy, we were ready to absorb ourselves in more spirituality in Mina, but first we had to get there! Luckily, we had heard on the grapevine that our group leader was going to attempt to find an empty bus that could take members of our group as close to our camp in Mina as possible. It was after midnight as we began the short walk to the area where most forms of public transported gathered – to call the area a bus stop or a taxi ramp would be misleading as they did not stop for the public – the public had to chase them in the hope that they would achieve a decent fare at a time when extortionate prices was the norm.

Small open-top trucks became temporary people carriers, but every attempt to flag them down failed. The group leader eventually negotiated a good price for an old, rickety bus that officially seated fifty passengers – our group at this point consisted of over eighty people, so several men were directed to the luggage rack on the roof of the bus and the rest of them stood in the aisle. Sweltering heat was now a habit and the lack of air conditioning wasn't even an issue – we were happy with the occasional warm breeze that helped us to cool down when the bus picked up speed.

Just as we entered Mina and the hundreds of thousands of tents came in to view, we were told to exit the bus – this was as far as the driver was prepared to go. The group leader pointed towards a steep, paved sidewalk that we were expected to climb – easy enough for the young amongst us but difficult for the more elderly pilgrims. Somehow, amidst the chaos, we managed to get everyone over the steep climb and began yet another short journey towards our tent. After an hour we arrived at the European camp and back on our sofa beds in the cool tent. It was approaching sunrise and as we waited the prayer time, we shared our experiences of the pilgrimage with each other. As soon as the beginning of prayer time came, we worshipped and then fell in to a deep sleep- re-booting our energy levels for another day full of praises towards Allah.

The next day, several of us had decided to walk towards the Satan wall together. There were many theories as to when would be the best time, however, we had learnt through experience that rather than using carefully analysed observations to predict when the pelting area would be 'quiet' it was more useful to rely on luck. When over two million people are all aiming to complete the same ritual in the same window of time it is impossible to predict how the public will make their decisions.

We chose to set off just before the time that pelting could begin – at midday, only to find that hundreds of thousands of people had decided to do the same thing, and so, we ended up ducking and diving through large crowds to get to the Satan walls. The experience of pelting was just as spiritual as the first time round, but now we also had adrenalin running through our bloodstream as we smiled at the organised chaos that surrounded us.

Once we had pelted all three walls that represented the three places where Ibrahim AS heard the whisperings of Satan, we re-grouped to make our way back to our tents in Mina.

The enthusiasm with which he had walked to the Satan walls was now flagging as we walked in the extreme heat of the day towards our tent. We considered it a blessing that we had become familiar with our surroundings and were not concerned about getting lost. A few of our group members had found themselves wandering amidst the many identical tests and it took them several hours to find their way back 'home'.

Eventually the familiar landmarks that reassured us that we were close comforted our eyes. Apart from our small independent group, none of the other pilgrims in our tents had yet been for the pelting. This was music to my ears as I knew that most of them would vacate the tent soon, leaving relative peace and quiet behind and an environment that was not congested with breathing bodies. After a late lunch, we engaged ourselves in prayer, grateful that we were to be rewarded with a peaceful rest later.

The next day, we left Mina for the final pelting after mid-day. The walk towards the Satan walls was relatively calm, as was the pelting itself, but the second half of the journey was highly congested. All the pilgrims were making their way back to Mecca and at times, we just stood lodged amongst the crowds as there was simply nowhere to go. Despite this, and the incredible heat, we were full of good spirits: that same sense of celebration that we felt as we were leaving for Mecca after the first pelting was again filling the air. We felt renewed. Something had changed in all of us. Allah had given us the opportunity to start again. We were re-born, sinless and determined to remain in a state that was pleasing to Allah.

The rest of our stay in Mecca, which was to be six more days, was spent completing numerous circumambulations of the Kabah and regular attendance of prayers at the mosque. Our days were still exhausting as we continued to battle with the heat and the relentless rush of pilgrims. Sleep patterns were irregular and interrupted as we adjusted to our sleep according to the prayer times. Looking at the Kabah was still an awe-inspiring experience – it exuded an aura of peace and tranquillity and Allah rewarded the onlooker with His blessings. I would search for a spot where I could achieve some sense of privacy amongst the hundreds of thousands of people surrounding me and then reflect upon the beginnings of the Kabah.

Allah asked Adam AS, the first man on earth, to build the Kabah as a house of worship towards Him. It was ordained by Allah that the Kabah be built in the shape of the House in Heaven called Baitul Ma'amoor. Allah, in his infinite Mercy, ordained a similar place on earth and Prophet Adam was the first to build this place. Ibrahim AS was then instructed to rebuild the Kabah on the foundations of the original one and to pronounce it as the house of worship. Together with his son Ismail AS the

Kabah was built and it still stands on the same spot today. The prophet Muhammad (peace be upon him), thousands of years later, was ordered by Allah to return the purpose of the Kabah back to its original role: a place for worshipping Allah alone as, throughout the centuries, it had been filled with idols that were worshipped along with Allah.

I tried to imagine how the prophets must have felt when they were given such a big privilege: what an honour to lay down the first stone, to construct the place of worship that millions turn to in their prayers. I envisaged the simplicity of the Kabah before the mosque around it was built and how much spirituality there must have been at the time of the prophets when there were no crowds – just a complete focus on what the Kabah represented and the utter, deep felt joy of feeling a connection with the Almighty. I had to work hard to get even a fraction of what they must have felt, but it was possible.

By ignoring the pushing and shoving and by thinking about the history of the Kabah and the fact that the angels were circumambulating the Kabah allowed my soul to open up to something beyond the earthly – I felt a shortness of breath and my hairs stood on end as Allah allowed my heart to open up to the feeling that cannot be explained through the words of this world alone.

During our stay in Mecca we spent some time visiting places of historical significance. From afar, we saw cave Hira at the summit of a mountain, where Allah revealed the beginnings of the Quran to the Prophet Muhammad (peace be upon him) through the Angel Gabriel (AS). Hundreds of people were climbing up the mountain to offer prayers and salutations. We also saw from afar the cave where Prophet Muhammad (peace be upon him) and his companion Abu Bakr RA remained in hiding for three days when being hunted down by the unbelievers. Our guide told us the story of how his companion demonstrated incredible loyalty and love towards the Prophet by covering up holes in the cave with his hands and feet to protect him from the cold. He even suffered snakebites for his beloved prophet. When they eventually left the cave, Allah immediately sent down the command for a spider to weave a large web outside the entrance giving the impression that no one had entered the cave for days.

We also drove through the blessed areas of Mina, Arafat and Muzdaliffah. Without the crowds of pilgrims, Mina looked like a vast area of pure white – thousands upon thousands of tents covering the landscape. Arafat and Muzdaliffah had been cleared of the man-made piles of waste that had been left behind and were now back to their original, deserted state. In Arafat, we climbed the small rocky hill that led to the place where Adam and Eve were re-united and also where the prophet Muhammad (peace be upon him) gave his last sermon. All these Islamically significant sites helped to bring my religion to life and further embedded my beliefs and values.

After a few more days filled with only worship, prayers and supplication towards the Almighty, we were to leave for the holy city of Medina. The coach was to arrive after the Morning Prayer so I had the chance to pay a final visit to the Kabah.

After saying my congregational morning prayer on the top floor I waited half an hour for the crowds to dissipate then made my way to the ground floor where I could have a full view of the Kabah. I could already feel the emotions overtaking my senses as I walked towards the holy shrine, reluctant to get closer knowing that this would be the last time I would feel its power to the fullest.

As I looked up at the Kabah's glory, my hands cupped towards it, I pleaded to Allah to bring me back to where my heart felt most at home. Then, for the last time in full view of the Kabah, I asked Allah to give my dad a long, healthy life and asked Him to give us the strength to accept the time when he returned to Him. With tears flowing, I prayed that my ignorance and arrogance that led to the neglect of prayers in the past could be forgiven. My heart was, for many years of my adult life, void of the central belief of

Islam: to live life with the intention to please Allah first because of one's love for Him. I begged Allah to continue to put the strength in my heart to live my life for Him, to please him and to accept His will.

I knew it was time to walk away, but my feet were rooted to the floor.

Staring at the Kabah, I continued to pray for my family and friends: pious children, good health, a peaceful death with the testification that there is no God but Allah and the prophet Muhammad (peace be upon him) is his messenger as the last words on my lips, a peaceful rest in the grave and an easy path towards, if Allah wills, paradise. These were prayers that many members of my family and community asked me to say on their behalf and as I thought of each and every one of them, I closed my eyes and held this final memory close to my heart.

With a deep breath I turned around and began to walk away. I could feel the Kabah's pull and had to fight the temptation to look towards it again. My prayers continued as I quickly walked back to the hotel. Despite feeling low, I was still looking forward to the spiritual journey ahead. Medina is the place where the prophet Muhammad's (peace be upon him) home, mosque and tomb can be found, as well as many historical sites. The crowds are not in such big numbers and the peace and tranquillity extends throughout the city.

Most of our group had returned back to the UK, having visited Medina before the Hajj period. The fifteen of us who were left sat comfortably on the forty-seater coach and began our journey to Medina. As soon as we passed the holy city's border we began to send a variety of salutations upon the prophet in Arabic, the basic one being translated as: peace be upon you oh prophet of Allah. Every salutation that we send upon the prophet is humbled with a response from the prophet himself and it is said by Allah that whoever sends salutations upon the prophet will have him intercede on their behalf on the day of judgement.

Narrated by Ibn Umar (ra) that the Prophet (Peace be upon him) said: *Whosoever visits my grave then my intercession becomes Wajib for him* [Sunnan al-Daraqutni Volume No. 2, Page No. 244, Imam al-Bayhaqi in Shu'ab al-Iman (3/490) and others]

Just as we entered the hotel in Medina, we heard the call for prayer from the prophet's mosque, which was just a stone's throw away. We rushed into our rooms, performed ablution and made our way to the mosque. There were still crowds to navigate but without the deep congestion that was commonplace in Mecca. The prophet's mosque was beautiful. It's white, marble courtyards spread outwards as far as the eye can see from the mosque itself, which consists of an enormous ground floor divided up in to sections with separate entrances for each area. It's many minarets tower over the hotels that surround it, leaving it to be the dominating feature of Medina, unlike Mecca, where the Kabah has been dwarfed by the clock tower: a skyscraper consisting of hotels and shopping complexes that is considered by many to be an intrusion of the Western world, albeit a Saudi government initiative. This domineering tower gives the impression, to those who have the insight, of an Islam losing its depth and meaning in a land that has always been considered a place purely for spirituality and reflection. It is also one of many signs indicating a nearness to the day of judgement as prophesised by the Prophet Muhammad:

When you see the holes dug in the mountains of Makah and you see the buildings reach beyond the mountains

After saying our prayers we walked around the courtyard, soaking in the calm, peaceful atmosphere. The struggle to walk from one area to the next, that we had grown accustomed to in Mecca, had come to an end. Medina revealed its character of warmth, mutual respect and a spirituality that extended beyond the walls of the mosque. It seemed that the whole city was celebrating the prophet Muhammad's (peace be upon him) character by adopting his manners and attitude.

At the centre of the mosque is the prophet Muhammad's (peace be upon him) tomb, home and original mosque. Despite the long journey from Mecca, we couldn't wait to visit the prophet's grave, so setting aside our state of fatigue, we made our way towards the green dome under which he lay.

Arif and I separated as men and women were to greet the prophet from different areas. As I approached the entrance, I realised that the need for patience hadn't quite been extinguished: there were hundreds of women waiting to send salutations upon the prophet (peace be upon him) and many of them seemed to be in a hurry to get there. I took a deep breath, settled down with my prayer books and made the conscious decision to exercise patience and self-control.

Narrated Abdullah Ibn Umar:

Allah's Messenger (peace be upon him) said: *Whoever visits my grave after my death it is same as him visiting me in my life* [Imam Tabrani in his Al-Kabir Volume No. 12, Page No. 291. Imam Bayhaqi in Sha'yb ul Iman Volume No. 3: Hadith #489]

Keeping the above Hadiths in mind, I reflected upon the fact that I was in the presence of the prophet Muhammad (peace be upon him) himself: the perfect role model that Allah presented to mankind. Utter respect and humility were required from all pilgrims and, as I sent an abundance of salutations upon the prophet and his companions who were buried alongside him. I tried to ignore the women who were disregarding the required code of conduct. Mis-education or ignorance – whatever the excuse, the behaviour of these women angered me and upset me deeply. From a purely Islamic perspective, we were in the presence of the prophet Muhammad (peace be upon him) and no matter how long the wait to reach his grave, we were to demonstrate nothing but respect and humility as he could sense the atmosphere around him and he was acknowledging every greeting of peace sent to him with a blessed response. Yet some women were running in the mosque, eager to get from one queue to the next. Others were screaming hysterically as they got closer to his grave and some were climbing over the ladies who were waiting patiently. A minority were also disregarding the women who were employed precisely for the purpose of crowd control by physically pushing them to the side.

These women had become so obsessed with avoiding the long wait that they had forgotten in whose presence they were blessed to be in. With tears in my eyes, I begged Allah for His mercy - to forgive this charade of female frenzy and accept the intention that lay in all our hearts: to be in the presence of the prophet, to send him salutations and to pray to Him that the prophet will intercede on our behalf on the day of judgement.

My daily visits to the prophet's grave gradually enabled me to develop some immunity to the sights and sounds that I had experienced in my first visit. My focus became stronger and I made the effort to feel close to the prophet, locking the serenity of his presence deep in to my heart so that I could recall its purity and power when I returned home.

Our week in Medina consisted of prayers in the mosque, visiting the prophet's grave and exploring historical sites. We had the opportunity to see several tombs of the prophet's companions and to stand where once were fought bloody battles in the name of Islam and offer prayers in the first mosque in Medina that was built by the prophets own hands.

We also spent some of our time fulfilling the duties of shopping for family: a frustrating chore but a necessary one. Ideally, I would have preferred to buy only dates and holy water – these were the traditional gifts that were given to family and friends and to visitors who came to hear about our Hajj experience once we returned home, however, the modern day pilgrim was expected to return with Jabbas (full length garments for men and women), prayer caps, prayer beads, prayer mats and other religious artefacts that were associated with the faith.

Our week in Medina soon came to an end and with it would come the end of the intense worshipping and glorifying of Allah. It would be impossible to continue devoting the time and heart to prayers in the manner that we had become accustomed to during our pilgrimage once we returned home: reality would inevitably take over. However, I was determined to lock the memories and the emotions that I experienced deep within my heart and recall these feelings when I did find the time to absorb myself in quality prayer back home.

I said goodbye for the final time to the blessed lands that I was so fortunate to visit. After over three weeks of sharing the same space with people from all over the world, I was looking forward to getting back to a familiar environment where I could take good manners and civilised queuing for granted!

Whilst on the internal flight from Medina to Jeddah we saw Medina from the skies: a glorious white light that dwarfed its surroundings. I continued to send salutations to the prophet Muhammad (peace be upon him) until the flight attendant announced that we had flown past the border of Medina. With saddened hearts, we took a final look at the holy land from the skies and prayed that Allah would bring us back to our spiritual home in the very near future.

Chapter Thirty-six

Past, present and future?

Religion has always been my guiding light throughout my life and in recent years has come to the forefront, absorbing my every thought and action. I have gained only positivity from its guidance and, whilst still enjoying my life with friends and family, I have realised the ultimate reason for my existence. There are many cynics out there who would argue that religion is simply a form of control and a suppressant that restricts enjoyment of the present world. I hope that I have answered those cynics to some extent, highlighting the reality of a spirituality that too often gets ignored by those who stubbornly refuse to accept its powerful existence and choose to live a life where only the material exists. Anger, love and fear are all emotions that we accept without question, yet we cannot hold them in our hands and touch them. God's existence can also be felt with the presence of spirituality: a deep connection with a love beyond the boundaries of earthly explanation. To allow ourselves to feel this love we have to be willing to open our hearts without prejudice.

Contrary to the media representation of Islam, adhering to the rules and regulations of the religion, especially as a woman, has not restricted my choices in life. My relationship with Arif is full of mutual respect and understanding and our roles in the home are defined by the same boundaries of a typical non-Muslim home. The main difference is that whatever decision I make, be it about my career, my social life, my family or my future, because my love for Allah exceeds the love I feel for people and possessions, I always put my faith first. Any decision that has pleasing Allah as its motivation, guarantees peace and serenity as His guidance can only lead to righteousness. My choices lead me to happiness, not just for myself but to all those involved in my life and ultimately, God willing, this will lead to a peaceful afterlife.

I have had the question put to me by a non-Muslim about my reaction if after I die, I found out that God does not exist? Will all this self-reflection and sacrifice not have been a waste of my life? My instant response was to point out the obvious fact that if there was no God, I would never find out, as after death, I would simply be worm food! Then I jumped to my defence by opposing her presumption that I was 'wasting' my life by believing in the unseen – I live a happy, fulfilling life with a deeply spiritual thread running through it, providing me with contentment and hope for a meaningful future.

Ultimately though, faith is personal choice. I cannot

imagine a life without God, but there will always be people who will never comprehend the concept of belief. What matters is that as human beings, we respect each other's viewpoints and learn to live amongst each other without making judgements. Islam is not just a religion but also an absolute way of life and there is no room for compromise in terms of its rulings and expectations. As it says in the Quran:

Say: O ye that reject Faith! I worship not that which ye worship, nor will ye worship that which I worship. And I will not worship that which ye have been wont to worship, nor will ye worship that which I worship. To you be your Way, and to me mine. (Quran, Surah Kafiroon)

Life, past and present, involved many more lessons learned and experiences gained that affected me from the inside and influenced my personality: I met people from all walks of life, who changed my perceptions and broke down stereotypes; holidays abroad introduced me to cultures and beliefs that, despite the vast differences in practice, still connected in spirituality; entertaining personalities warmed my heart and made me laugh till tears streamed from my eyes; loving relationships have overwhelmed me with support and friendship and the unconditional love of my parents, that of my heroic mum, and the indirect yet strong love of my late father, has given me the gift of a soft heart that despises any form of confrontation or conflict.

My dad's departure from the world has left me with a sense of emptiness, yet his legacy, both the negative and the positive, has determined my strength in character and enabled me to use my intellect precisely how my dad intended. Even in his last days, my dad's faith and acceptance ensured that he continued his role as a father figure by allowing the strengthening of my own spirituality through his pain and suffering.

Although my dad was aware of the inclusion of his past in my work, it was not an easy decision to reveal his destructive nature, as Allah asks his followers to hide the sins of their fellow believers. However, my intention is to dispel misconceptions within both the Muslim and non-Muslim community concerning Islam's perception of violence in the home – the bigger purpose which I pray God will accept.

The hero of my story, my mum, continues to defend my dad. She is aware of what I have written and accepts the reasoning behind it; however she refuses to think ill of my dad. Despite her suffering, she understands and forgives her husband's actions wholeheartedly, accepting that outside of the violence, he had a loving heart that brought joy and strength to all those around him.

I have also attempted to break down the pre-conceptions of religion within a culture that has misconstrued its message. I have lived my life through a series of contradictions, but with my renewed faith and expanding knowledge, I am hoping that these contradictions will be eradicated from my life, allowing an existence based purely on religion.

Forty years however is impossible to express in a mere seventy thousand words. The objective of my condensed attempt was to share the many moments of happiness that we all experience at some point of our lives together with the times that challenge every part of our being, from the physical to the spiritual.

And as I look forward to a peaceful future, I pray that my intentions are accepted. My words come from the heart and my memories are genuine moments in my life that have made me who I am. The reader may now choose to discard the words as a source of short term entertainment or ponder upon them, bringing a small, positive change in to their lives and perhaps leading them to a life of faith, whatever that faith might be. All I ask is that the reader accepts my words as sincere, expressing a life full of lessons learned and conveying a journey of spirituality that eventually moulded my identity. I now look forward to a future that promises to remain faithful to my innermost beliefs and convictions and pray that the reader also has the strength to remain true to theirs.

Ameen